most loved recipe collection most loved recipe collection

Most Loved

Most Loved Barbecuing

by Jean Paré

most loved recipe collection

most
loved

barbecuing

Pictured on divider:
Top: Teriyaki Ribs, page 66
Bottom: Vegetable Skewers With Pesto Dressing, page 105

We gratefully acknowledge the following suppliers for their generous support of our
Test and Photography Kitchens:

Broil King Barbecues
Corelle®
Hamilton Beach ® Canada
Lagostina®
Proctor Silex ® Canada
Tupperware®

Our special thanks to the following businesses for providing props for photography:

Anchor Hocking Canada
Canhome Global
Casa Bugatti
Cherison Enterprises Inc.
Chintz & Company
Danesco Inc.
Emile Henry
Island Pottery Inc.
Klass Works
La Cache
Le Gnome
Linens 'N Things
Mikasa Home Store
Out of the Fire Studio
Pfaltzgraff Canada
Pier 1 Imports
Sears Canada
Stokes
The Bay
The Dazzling Gourmet
Tile Town
Totally Bamboo
Tupperware®
Wal-Mart Canada Inc.
Wiltshire®
Winners
X/S Wares
Zenari's

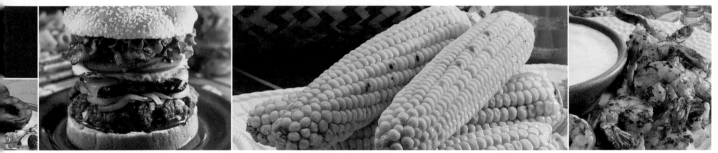

Pictured from left: Balsamic Peaches, page 114; Super Oz Burgers, page 46; Quick Corn, page 102; Barbecued Shrimp, page 14.

table of contents

"Never share a recipe you wouldn't use yourself"

the Company's Coming story

Jean Paré (pronounced "jeen PAIR-ee") grew up understanding that the combination of family, friends and home cooking is the best recipe for a good life. From her mother, she learned to appreciate good cooking, while her father praised even her earliest attempts in the kitchen. When Jean left home, she took with her a love of cooking, many family recipes and an intriguing desire to read cookbooks as if they were novels!

When her four children had all reached school age, Jean volunteered to cater the 50th anniversary celebration of the Vermilion School of Agriculture, now Lakeland College, in Alberta, Canada. Working out of her home, Jean prepared a dinner for more than 1,000 people, launching a flourishing catering operation that continued for over 18 years. During that time, she had countless opportunities to test new ideas with immediate feedback—resulting in empty plates and contented customers! Whether preparing cocktail sandwiches for a house party or serving a hot meal for 1,500 people, Jean Paré earned a reputation for great food, courteous service and reasonable prices.

As requests for her recipes increased, Jean was often asked the question, "Why don't you write a cookbook?" Jean responded by teaming up with her son, Grant Lovig, in the fall of 1980 to form Company's Coming Publishing Limited. The publication of *150 Delicious Squares* on April 14, 1981 marked the debut of what would soon become one of the world's most popular cookbook series.

The company has grown since those early days when Jean worked from a spare bedroom in her home. Today, she continues to write recipes while working closely with the staff of the Recipe Factory, as the Company's Coming test kitchen is affectionately known. There she fills the role of mentor, assisting with the development of recipes people most want to use for everyday cooking and easy entertaining. Every Company's Coming recipe is kitchen-tested before it is approved for publication.

Jean's daughter, Gail Lovig, is responsible for marketing and distribution, leading a team that includes sales personnel located in major cities across Canada. Company's Coming cookbooks are distributed in Canada, the United States, Australia and other world markets. Bestsellers many times over in English, Company's Coming cookbooks have also been published in French and Spanish.

Familiar and trusted in home kitchens around the world, Company's Coming cookbooks are offered in a variety of formats. Highly regarded as kitchen workbooks, the softcover Original Series, with its lay-flat plastic comb binding, is still a favourite among readers.

Jean Paré's approach to cooking has always called for quick and easy recipes using everyday ingredients. That view has served her well. The recipient of many awards, including the Queen Elizabeth Golden Jubilee Medal, Jean was appointed Member of the Order of Canada, her country's highest lifetime achievement honour.

Jean continues to gain new supporters by adhering to what she calls The Golden Rule of Cooking: *Never share a recipe you wouldn't use yourself.* It's an approach that has worked—millions of times over!

foreword

You'll never be at a loss for something delicious to grill with *Most Loved Barbecuing*. Leaf through pages of time-tested, beautifully photographed, consistently delicious recipes that use ingredients you already have on hand.

Though we can barbecue year-round, with the approach of summer, we rush to our outdoor grills for the great taste of something smoked and sizzling. Barbecuing isn't only for steaks, burgers or potatoes—though sometimes nothing could be better! It's also for baking muffins, cakes or bread, grilling vegetables or fruit, or cooking roasts and ribs. You can prepare appetizers, side dishes, entrées and desserts using this one versatile appliance, without all those extra pots and pans to clean later. For even easier cleanup, use foil and foil pans.

When you barbecue, it feels less like work and more like taking the time to grill a meal you'll enjoy with your family and friends. And because you aren't stuck in the kitchen, you can join the party while grilling something tantalizing.

Don't forget to add extra flavour to your meat with a spicy rub or marinade, or complement your meal with a delicious sauce or dip, crisp salad, fresh vegetables or fruit. The contrast between the hot food coming off the barbecue and the cool food from the refrigerator will please your palate. Be close by when the cook calls because you won't want to miss a bite!

We've included recipes that use direct and indirect cooking methods. For indirect cooking, the burner under the food is turned off and the opposite burner is left on. The lid is always closed to maintain an even heat for cooking such foods as pies, cakes, breads, Yorkshire pudding, meat and poultry. We've also compiled helpful hints to ensure your barbecuing success. All recipes have been tested on a gas barbecue.

Whether it's vegetables or fruit, breads or buns, fish or poultry, beef or pork, *Most Loved Barbecuing* helps you grill it to perfection. So, get out of the kitchen and into the great outdoors. It's a perfect time to put some sizzle into all your favourite meals!

Jean Paré

nutrition information guidelines

Each recipe is analyzed using the most current version of the Canadian Nutrient File from Health Canada, which is based on the United States Department of Agriculture (USDA) Nutrient Database.

- If more than one ingredient is listed (such as "hard margarine or butter"), or if a range is given (1 – 2 tsp., 5 – 10 mL), only the first ingredient or first amount is analyzed.

- For meat, poultry and fish, the serving size per person is based on the recommended 4 oz. (113 g) uncooked weight (without bone), which is 2 – 3 oz. (57 – 85 g) cooked weight (without bone)— approximately the size of a deck of playing cards.

- Milk used is 1% M.F. (milk fat), unless otherwise stated.

- Cooking oil used is canola oil, unless otherwise stated.

- Ingredients indicating "sprinkle," "optional," or "for garnish" are not included in the nutrition information.

Margaret Ng, B.Sc. (Hon), M.A.
Registered Dietitian

Red wine and mustard are classic marinade partners, especially when teamed with garlic and pepper, as in this recipe.

Red Wine, Mustard And Garlic Marinade

Dry red (or alcohol-free) wine	1 cup	250 mL
Dijon mustard (with whole seeds)	2 tbsp.	30 mL
Barbecue sauce (your favourite)	2 tbsp.	30 mL
Worcestershire sauce	1 tbsp.	15 mL
Olive (or cooking) oil	1 tbsp.	15 mL
Garlic cloves, minced (or 1 tsp., 5 mL, powder)	4	4
Pepper	1 tsp.	5 mL

Combine all 7 ingredients in small bowl. Makes about 1 1/3 cups (325 mL).

1 tbsp. (15 mL): 17 Calories; 0.7 g Total Fat (0.5 g Mono, 0.1 g Poly, 0.1 g Sat); 0 mg Cholesterol; 1 g Carbohydrate; trace Fibre; 0 g Protein; 39 mg Sodium

Pictured on page 7.

This combination of lively spices is tempered nicely by the addition of fresh herbs.

Spice And Herb Marinade

Orange juice	1/2 cup	125 mL
Dry white (or alcohol-free) wine	1/2 cup	125 mL
Chopped fresh cilantro or parsley (or 1 tbsp., 15 mL, dried)	1/4 cup	60 mL
Chopped fresh mint leaves (or 1 tbsp., 15 mL, dried)	1/4 cup	60 mL
Olive (or cooking) oil	2 tbsp.	30 mL
Liquid honey	2 tbsp.	30 mL
Garlic cloves, minced (or 1/2 tsp., 2 mL, powder)	2	2
Grated orange zest	1 tsp.	5 mL
Ground cumin	1 tsp.	5 mL
Ground cinnamon	1/2 tsp.	2 mL
Ground ginger	1/2 tsp.	2 mL
Chili powder	1/4 tsp.	1 mL

Combine all 12 ingredients in small bowl. Makes about 1 1/3 cups (325 mL).

1 tbsp. (15 mL): 25 Calories; 1.3 g Total Fat (0.9 g Mono, 0.1 g Poly, 0.2 g Sat); 0 mg Cholesterol; 3 g Carbohydrate; trace Fibre; 0 g Protein; 1 mg Sodium

Pictured on page 7.

Top Right: Spice And Herb Marinade, above
Bottom Left: Red Wine, Mustard And Garlic Marinade, above

Look no further for the world's greatest steak sauce. Mildly spiced and creamy. Perfect for a juicy grilled T-bone or porterhouse steak.

Green Peppercorn Sauce

Hard margarine (or butter)	1 tbsp.	15 mL
Small onion, finely chopped	1	1
Garlic cloves, minced (or 1/2 tsp., 2 mL, powder)	2	2
Brandy	2 tbsp.	30 mL
Whipping cream	1 1/2 cups	375 mL
Can of green peppercorns in brine, drained	1 oz.	30 g
Prepared mustard	1 tsp.	5 mL
Salt	1/4 tsp.	1 mL

Melt margarine in large frying pan on medium. Add onion. Cook for 5 to 10 minutes, stirring often, until softened.

Add garlic. Heat and stir for 1 to 2 minutes until fragrant. Add brandy. Immediately ignite with match to burn off alcohol.

Add remaining 4 ingredients. Heat and stir for 5 to 10 minutes until boiling and slightly thickened. Makes about 1 1/2 cups (375 mL).

1 tbsp. (15 mL): 54 Calories; 5.3 g Total Fat (1.7 g Mono, 0.2 g Poly, 3.1 g Sat); 18 mg Cholesterol; 1 g Carbohydrate; trace Fibre; 0 g Protein; 38 mg Sodium

Pictured on page 9.

A mild marinade. Great for shrimp or other seafood.

Lemon Marinade

Cooking oil	1/2 cup	125 mL
Juice and sliced peel of small lemon	1	1
Dried thyme	1/2 tsp.	2 mL
Garlic powder	1/4 tsp.	1 mL
Seasoned salt	1/4 tsp.	1 mL
Salt	1/4 tsp.	1 mL
Pepper, sprinkle		
Hot pepper sauce (optional)	1/8 tsp.	0.5 mL

Combine all 8 ingredients in small bowl. Makes about 3/4 cup (175 mL).

1 tbsp. (15 mL): 84 Calories; 9.2 g Total Fat (5.4 g Mono, 2.7 g Poly, 0.7 g Sat); 0 mg Cholesterol; 1 g Carbohydrate; trace Fibre; 0 g Protein; 72 mg Sodium

Pictured on page 9.

Left: Green Peppercorn Sauce, above
Right: Lemon Marinade, above

Plan an Indian-style barbecue using this basting sauce to add great flavour to beef. Use a hotter curry paste if you prefer more spice.

Curried Yogurt Basting Sauce

Plain yogurt	1 1/4 cups	300 mL
Curry paste	1/4 cup	60 mL
Chopped fresh mint leaves (or 1 tbsp., 15 mL, dried)	1/4 cup	60 mL
Chopped fresh cilantro or parsley (or 1 tbsp., 15 mL, dried)	1/4 cup	60 mL
Mango chutney	2 tbsp.	30 mL

Combine all 5 ingredients in medium bowl. Makes about 1 1/2 cups (375 mL).

1 tbsp. (15 mL): 21 Calories; 1.4 g Total Fat (0.7 g Mono, 0.3 g Poly, 0.2 g Sat); 1 mg Cholesterol; 2 g Carbohydrate; trace Fibre; 1 g Protein; 10 mg Sodium

Pictured on page 11.

A versatile sauce—tastes great with beef, chicken, fish or pork.

Fast Teriyaki Sauce

Soy sauce	1/2 cup	125 mL
Cooking oil	1/4 cup	60 mL
Ketchup	1 tbsp.	15 mL
Garlic powder	1/4 tsp.	1 mL

Combine all 4 ingredients in small bowl. Makes about 3/4 cup (175 mL).

1 tbsp. (15 mL): 50 Calories; 4.6 g Total Fat (2.7 g Mono, 1.4 g Poly, 0.3 g Sat); 0 mg Cholesterol; 1 g Carbohydrate; trace Fibre; 1 g Protein; 709 mg Sodium

Pictured on page 11.

Top Right: Curried Yogurt Basting Sauce, above
Bottom Left: Fast Teriyaki Sauce, above

Herbs and spice are always nice. Give them a shake — try them rubbed on steak.

make ahead

Double or triple your favourite rub recipe and store in an airtight container. Rub any of these savoury combinations on both sides of steaks, or sprinkle on burgers, before grilling. Use as much or as little as you like.

Steak Rubs

LEMON PEPPER RUB

Garlic powder	1 tsp.	5 mL
Lemon pepper	1 tsp.	5 mL
Grated lemon zest	1/2 tsp.	2 mL
Dried basil	1/2 tsp.	2 mL

Combine all 4 ingredients in small cup. Makes about 1 tbsp. (15 mL).

1/2 tsp. (2 mL): 2 Calories; 0 g Total Fat (0 g Mono, 0 g Poly, 0 g Sat); 0 mg Cholesterol; 1 g Carbohydrate; trace Fibre; 0 g Protein; 198 mg Sodium

Pictured on page 13.

HERB AND SPICE RUB

Parsley flakes, crushed	1 tbsp.	15 mL
Paprika	1 tsp.	5 mL
Garlic powder	1 tsp.	5 mL
Pepper	1/4 tsp.	1 mL

Combine all 4 ingredients in small cup. Makes about 1 1/2 tbsp. (25 mL).

1/2 tsp. (2 mL): 2 Calories; 0 g Total Fat (0 g Mono, 0 g Poly, 0 g Sat); 0 mg Cholesterol; 0 g Carbohydrate; trace Fibre; 0 g Protein; 1 mg Sodium

Pictured on page 13.

CHILI RUB

Onion powder	1 tsp.	5 mL
Chili powder	1 tsp.	5 mL
Garlic salt	1 tsp.	5 mL
Dried whole oregano, crushed	1 tsp.	5 mL
Ground cumin	1 tsp.	5 mL

Combine all 5 ingredients in small cup. Makes about 1 1/2 tbsp. (25 mL).

1/2 tsp. (2 mL): 4 Calories; 0.1 g Total Fat (0 g Mono, 0 g Poly, 0 g Sat); 0 mg Cholesterol; 1 g Carbohydrate; trace Fibre; 0 g Protein; 135 mg Sodium

Pictured on page 13.

(continued on next page)

NEW ORLEANS RUB

Garlic salt	1 tsp.	5 mL
Curry powder	1 tsp.	5 mL
Paprika	1 tsp.	5 mL
Cayenne pepper	1/4 tsp.	1 mL

Combine all 4 ingredients in small cup. Makes about 1 tbsp. (15 mL).

1/2 tsp. (2 mL): *3 Calories; 0.1 g Total Fat (0 g Mono, 0 g Poly, 0 g Sat); 0 mg Cholesterol; 1 g Carbohydrate; trace Fibre; 0 g Protein; 198 mg Sodium*

Pictured below.

Top Left: Lemon Pepper Rub, page 12
Top Right: Chili Rub, page 12
Bottom Left: Herb And Spice Rub, page 12
Bottom Right: New Orleans Rub, this page

Perfectly marinated and barbecued shrimp served with a rich garlic mayonnaise.

make ahead

The Garlic Mayonnaise can be made 1 or 2 days ahead. Store in airtight container in refrigerator.

Barbecued Shrimp

GARLIC MAYONNAISE		
Large egg	1	1
Egg yolk (large)	1	1
Lemon juice	1 tbsp.	15 mL
Garlic clove, minced (or 1/4 tsp., 1 mL, powder)	1	1
Salt	1/8 tsp.	0.5 mL
Cooking oil	3/4 cup	175 mL
SEAFOOD MARINADE		
Chopped fresh parsley (or 2 1/4 tsp., 11 mL, flakes)	3 tbsp.	50 mL
Cooking oil	2 tbsp.	30 mL
Grated lemon zest	1/2 tsp.	2 mL
Salt	1/2 tsp.	2 mL
Pepper	1/2 tsp.	2 mL
Fresh uncooked jumbo shrimp (tails intact), peeled and deveined	18	18

Garlic Mayonnaise: Process first 5 ingredients in blender or food processor for about 2 minutes until creamy.

With motor running, slowly pour first amount of cooking oil through hole in lid until mixture is pale and thickened. Transfer to small bowl. Cover with plastic wrap. Chill for at least 1 hour to blend flavours. Makes about 1 cup (250 mL) mayonnaise.

Seafood Marinade: Combine next 5 ingredients in medium bowl. Makes about 1/3 cup (75 mL) marinade.

Add shrimp. Toss until coated. Cover with plastic wrap. Marinate in refrigerator for at least 1 hour, stirring occasionally. Drain and discard marinade. Preheat barbecue to medium. Cook shrimp on greased grill for about 5 minutes, turning occasionally, until shrimp are pink. Do not overcook. Serve with Garlic Mayonnaise. Serves 6.

1 serving: 364 Calories; 33.9 g Total Fat (19.2 g Mono, 9.9 g Poly, 2.9 g Sat); 163 mg Cholesterol; 1 g Carbohydrate; trace Fibre; 14 g Protein; 251 mg Sodium

Pictured on page 15.

Bulgogi (bul-GO-gee) is a popular Korean beef dish. Makes a great appetizer for a summer patio party.

notes

To toast seeds, spread evenly in ungreased shallow pan. Bake in 350°F (175°C) oven for 5 to 10 minutes, stirring or shaking often, until desired doneness.

To slice meat easily, place in freezer for about 30 minutes until just beginning to freeze. If using from frozen state, partially thaw before slicing.

Bulgogi Vegetable Bundles

BULGOGI MARINADE

Indonesian sweet (or thick) soy sauce	1/4 cup	60 mL
Water	1/4 cup	60 mL
Cooking oil	1 tbsp.	15 mL
Dry sherry	1 tbsp.	15 mL
Garlic cloves, minced (or 1/2 tsp., 2 mL, powder)	2	2
Green onion, cut into 4 pieces	1	1
Sesame seeds, toasted (see Note)	2 tsp.	10 mL
Flank steak, cut diagonally into 1/8 inch (3 mm) thick slices (see Note)	3/4 lb.	340 g
Steamed whole carrots, cut into 4 inch (10 cm) lengths, quartered lengthwise	4	4
Steamed fresh asparagus (or whole green beans), cut into 4 inch (10 cm) lengths	10	10
Roasted red peppers, cut into 4 inch (10 cm) strips	2	2
Lightly steamed medium zucchini (with peel), cut lengthwise into 8 pieces, then into 4 inch (10 cm) lengths	1	1
Bamboo skewers (8 inch, 20 cm, length), soaked in water for 10 minutes	20	20

Bulgogi Marinade: Process first 7 ingredients in blender or food processor until smooth. Makes about 3/4 cup (175 mL) marinade. Pour into large resealable freezer bag.

Add steak slices. Seal bag. Turn until coated. Marinate in refrigerator for at least 2 hours, turning occasionally. Drain and discard marinade.

Divide and layer vegetables crosswise on steak slices. Roll up into bundles. Thread 2 bundles onto 2 skewers, ladder-style. Preheat barbecue to medium. Cook bundles on greased grill for about 2 1/2 minutes per side until steak slices are cooked to desired doneness. Serves 10.

1 serving: 98 Calories; 4 g Total Fat (1.7 g Mono, 0.5 g Poly, 1.4 g Sat); 14 mg Cholesterol; 7 g Carbohydrate; 2 g Fibre; 9 g Protein; 199 mg Sodium

Pictured on pages 18/19.

Tandoori Pork Bites

Plain yogurt	2/3 cup	150 mL
Tandoori paste	1/2 cup	125 mL
Mango chutney	1/3 cup	75 mL
Pork tenderloin, trimmed of fat, cut into 3/4 inch (2 cm) cubes	1 lb.	454 g
Bamboo skewers (8 inch, 20 cm, length), soaked in water for 10 minutes	8	8
MANGO YOGURT DIP		
Plain yogurt	1/2 cup	125 mL
Mango chutney	1/3 cup	75 mL

Combine first 3 ingredients in large bowl. Makes about 1 1/2 cups (375 mL) marinade.

Add pork. Stir until coated. Cover with plastic wrap. Marinate in refrigerator for at least 6 hours or overnight, stirring occasionally. Drain and discard marinade.

Thread 4 pork cubes onto each skewer. Preheat barbecue to medium. Cook skewers on greased grill for 5 to 7 minutes, turning occasionally, until pork is no longer pink inside.

Mango Yogurt Dip: Combine yogurt and chutney in small bowl. Makes about 1 cup (250 mL) dip. Serve with pork bites. Makes 8 skewers.

1 skewer with 2 tbsp. (30 mL) dip: 113 Calories; 1.9 g Total Fat (0.8 g Mono, 0.2 g Poly, 0.8 g Sat); 35 mg Cholesterol; 9 g Carbohydrate; trace Fibre; 15 g Protein; 197 mg Sodium

Pictured on page 18.

The yogurt dip cools these spicy bite-size appetizers.

Photo Legend, next page

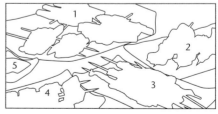

1. Bulgogi Vegetable Bundles, page 16
2. Satay, page 20
3. Korean Skewered Pork, page 21
4. Tandoori Pork Bites, this page
5. Mango Yogurt Dip, this page

Tender sirloin gently barbecued to flavourful perfection. You'll crave this.

note

To slice meat easily, place in freezer for about 30 minutes until just beginning to freeze. If using from frozen state, partially thaw before slicing.

Satay

SATAY MARINADE

Soy sauce	2/3 cup	150 mL
Granulated sugar	1/3 cup	75 mL
Ketchup	2 tbsp.	30 mL
Cooking oil	2 tbsp.	30 mL
Ground ginger	1/2 tsp.	2 mL
Garlic powder	1/4 tsp.	1 mL
Onion powder	1/4 tsp.	1 mL
Beef sirloin tip roast, thinly cut across the grain (see Note)	1 1/2 lbs.	680 g
Bamboo skewers (8 inch, 20 cm, length), soaked in water for 10 minutes	6	6

Satay Marinade: Combine first 7 ingredients in large bowl. Makes about 1 cup (250 mL) marinade.

Cut beef slices into 1 1/2 to 2 inch (3.8 to 5 cm) long strips. Add beef to marinade. Stir until coated. Cover with plastic wrap. Marinate in refrigerator for at least 30 minutes, stirring occasionally. Drain and discard marinade.

Thread beef, accordion-style, onto skewers. Preheat barbecue to medium-high. Cook skewers on greased grill for 4 to 5 minutes, turning occasionally, until desired doneness. Makes 6 skewers.

1 skewer: 218 Calories; 8.2 g Total Fat (3.9 g Mono, 1 g Poly, 2.3 g Sat); 54 mg Cholesterol; 8 g Carbohydrate; trace Fibre; 27 g Protein; 1074 mg Sodium

Pictured on page 19.

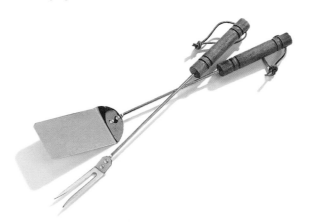

Korean Skewered Pork

SWEET CHILI MARINADE

Low-sodium soy sauce	1/3 cup	75 mL
Sweet chili sauce	1/4 cup	60 mL
Sesame oil, for flavour	1 tbsp.	15 mL
Sesame seeds, toasted (see Note)	1 tbsp.	15 mL
Garlic cloves, minced (or 1 tsp., 5 mL, powder)	4	4
Brown sugar, packed	2 tsp.	10 mL
Finely grated, peeled gingerroot (or 1/4 tsp., 1 mL, ground ginger)	1 tsp.	5 mL
Chili paste (sambal oelek)	1 tsp.	5 mL
Boneless pork shoulder butt roast, cut diagonally into 1/8 inch (3 mm) thick slices (see Note)	1 1/2 lbs.	680 g
Bamboo skewers (8 inch, 20 cm, length), soaked in water for 10 minutes	12	12

Sweet Chili Marinade: Combine first 8 ingredients in small bowl. Makes about 3/4 cup (175 mL) marinade. Pour into large resealable freezer bag.

Add pork. Seal bag. Turn until coated. Marinate in refrigerator for at least 6 hours or overnight, turning occasionally. Drain and discard marinade.

Thread pork loosely, accordion-style, onto skewers. Preheat barbecue to medium-high. Cook skewers on greased grill for 5 to 7 minutes per side until pork is no longer pink. Makes 12 skewers.

1 skewer: 152 Calories; 11.2 g Total Fat (4.9 g Mono, 1.4 g Poly, 3.7 g Sat); 34 mg Cholesterol; 2 g Carbohydrate; trace Fibre; 11 g Protein; 188 mg Sodium

Pictured on page 19.

Tasty skewers with a mild ginger and sesame flavour. For thin pork slices, ask your butcher to slice the roast with a meat cutter.

notes

To toast seeds, spread evenly in ungreased shallow pan. Bake in 350°F (175°C) oven for 5 to 10 minutes, stirring or shaking often, until desired doneness.

To slice meat easily, place in freezer for about 30 minutes until just beginning to freeze. If using from frozen state, partially thaw before slicing.

Small toasted bread rounds topped with sweet roasted peppers and feta cheese. It's bruschetta with a Greek twist.

Red Pepper Bruschetta

Red medium pepper, quartered, seeds and ribs removed	1	1
Yellow medium pepper, quartered, seeds and ribs removed	1	1
Finely chopped fresh parsley (or 1 1/2 tsp., 7 mL, flakes)	2 tbsp.	30 mL
Finely chopped red onion	2 tbsp.	30 mL
Olive (or cooking) oil	1 tbsp.	15 mL
Red wine vinegar	2 tsp.	10 mL
Granulated sugar	1/2 tsp.	2 mL
Salt	1/4 tsp.	1 mL
Pepper, just a pinch		
Baguette bread loaf (about 24 inch, 60 cm, length), cut diagonally into 1/2 inch (12 mm) thick slices	1	1
Olive (or cooking) oil	2 tbsp.	30 mL
Garlic clove, halved	1	1
Crumbled feta cheese	1 cup	250 mL

Preheat barbecue to high. Arrange red and yellow peppers, skin-side down, on greased grill. Cook for 10 to 15 minutes until skins are blistered and blackened. Remove to medium bowl. Cover with plastic wrap. Let sweat for about 15 minutes until cool enough to handle. Peel and discard skins. Chop finely. Return to same bowl.

Add next 7 ingredients. Stir. Cover with plastic wrap. Chill for at least 1 hour, stirring occasionally, to blend flavours. Makes about 1 cup (250 mL) pepper mixture.

Reduce barbecue heat to low. Brush both sides of baguette slices with second amount of olive oil. Place slices on grill. Toast both sides until lightly browned.

Rub 1 side of each baguette slice with garlic clove. Divide and spoon pepper mixture on top.

Sprinkle feta cheese over top of pepper mixture on each slice. Makes about 30 bruschetta.

1 bruschetta: 51 Calories; 2.8 g Total Fat (1.4 g Mono, 0.2 g Poly, 1.1 g Sat); 5 mg Cholesterol; 5 g Carbohydrate; trace Fibre; 2 g Protein; 127 mg Sodium

Pictured on page 23.

Have these for a quick snack when you're in the mood for something cheesy and crispy.

serving suggestion

Serve with sour cream and salsa, along with an icy cold glass of your favourite summer punch.

variation

Place sheet of heavy-duty (or double layer of regular) foil on baking sheet. Grease foil with cooking spray. Crowd chips into 1 large circle. Cook as directed.

Pictured on page 25.

Nachos

Bag of corn (or tortilla) chips	9 oz.	240 g
Grated Monterey Jack cheese	1 1/4 cups	300 mL
Grated medium Cheddar cheese	1 1/4 cups	300 mL
Bacon slices, cooked crisp and crumbled	6	6
Can of diced green chilies	4 oz.	113 g
Green onions, sliced	3	3

Cut six 12 inch (30 cm) squares of heavy-duty (or double layer of regular) foil. Grease each square with cooking spray. Arrange chips in 6 inch (15 cm) circle on each square. Crowd chips together so little or no foil is visible through them.

Divide and layer remaining 5 ingredients, in order given, on top of chips. Preheat barbecue to medium-low. Place squares on ungreased grill. Close lid. Cook for 5 to 10 minutes until cheese is melted. Check often, as they burn easily. Serves 6.

1 serving: 335 Calories; 21.2 g Total Fat (9.9 g Mono, 2.1 g Poly, 7.9 g Sat); 28 mg Cholesterol; 27 g Carbohydrate; 3 g Fibre; 11 g Protein; 447 mg Sodium

You haven't had pizza until you've had it made on the barbecue! Add any deli meats you like for your own unique touch.

birthday pizza

Arrange strips of green or red pepper on top of pizza in the shape of the number that represents the birthday year!

Pizza On The Grill

Biscuit mix	2 cups	500 mL
Milk	1/2 cup	125 mL
Pasta (or pizza) sauce	1 cup	250 mL
Grated part-skim mozzarella cheese	2 cups	500 mL
Sliced fresh white mushrooms	1 cup	250 mL
Chopped deli meat (your favourite)	1 cup	250 mL
Chopped green onion	1/2 cup	125 mL
Chopped red pepper	1/2 cup	125 mL
Grated part-skim mozzarella cheese	1 cup	250 mL

Measure biscuit mix into medium bowl. Add milk. Stir until just moistened. Turn out dough onto lightly floured surface. Knead 8 to 10 times. Press evenly in greased 12 inch (30 cm) pizza pan. Preheat barbecue to high. Place pan on 1 side of ungreased grill. Turn off burner under pan, turning opposite burner down to medium. Close lid. Cook for about 15 minutes, rotating pan at halftime, until crust is just starting to turn golden.

Spread pasta sauce evenly over crust.

Layer next 5 ingredients, in order given, over sauce.

Sprinkle with second amount of mozzarella cheese. Return to unlit side of grill. Close lid. Cook for about 15 minutes until heated through and cheese is melted. Cuts into 6 wedges.

1 wedge: 481 Calories; 22.9 g Total Fat (8.1 g Mono, 4 g Poly, 9.3 g Sat); 57 mg Cholesterol; 41 g Carbohydrate; 1 g Fibre; 27 g Protein; 1560 mg Sodium

Pictured on page 27.

These are a welcome change from bread or dinner rolls for any barbecued meal.

serving suggestion

These muffins are perfect as a side served with Java Ribs, page 97, and Foiled Yams, page 109.

dotted corn muffins

Add 3 tbsp. (50 mL) chopped green onion and 2 tbsp. (30 mL) each of chopped green pepper and red pepper to egg mixture before adding to well.

Corn Muffins

All-purpose flour	1 1/4 cups	300 mL
Yellow cornmeal	3/4 cup	175 mL
Granulated sugar	1/4 cup	60 mL
Baking powder	2 tsp.	10 mL
Salt	1/2 tsp.	2 mL
Plain yogurt	1 cup	250 mL
Cooking oil	1/4 cup	60 mL
Large egg	1	1

Measure first 5 ingredients into large bowl. Stir. Make a well in centre.

Combine remaining 3 ingredients in small bowl. Add to well. Stir until just moistened. Grease 12 muffin cups with cooking spray. Fill cups 3/4 full. Preheat barbecue to high. Place muffin pan on 1 side of ungreased grill. Turn off burner under muffin pan, turning opposite burner down to medium. Close lid. Cook for 20 to 25 minutes, rotating pan at halftime, until muffins are golden and wooden pick inserted in centre of muffin comes out clean. Let stand in pan for 5 minutes before removing to wire rack to cool. Makes 12 muffins.

1 muffin: 164 Calories; 5.9 g Total Fat (3.2 g Mono, 1.6 g Poly, 0.7 g Sat); 19 mg Cholesterol; 24 g Carbohydrate; 1 g Fibre; 4 g Protein; 182 mg Sodium

Pictured on pages 30/31.

Blueberry Muffins

A delicious treat for a barbecue brunch.

Hard margarine (or butter), softened	1/4 cup	60 mL
Granulated sugar	1/4 cup	60 mL
Large egg	1	1
All-purpose flour	1 3/4 cups	425 mL
Baking powder	4 tsp.	20 mL
Grated lemon zest	1 tsp.	5 mL
Salt	1/2 tsp.	2 mL
Milk	1 cup	250 mL
Fresh (or frozen, thawed) blueberries	1 cup	250 mL
All-purpose flour	1/4 cup	60 mL

Cream margarine and sugar in large bowl. Add egg. Beat until smooth.

Combine next 4 ingredients in medium bowl.

Add flour mixture to margarine mixture in 3 additions, alternating with milk in 2 additions, beginning and ending with flour mixture, stirring after each addition until just moistened.

Measure blueberries into small bowl. Sprinkle with second amount of flour. Toss gently until coated. Add to batter. Stir gently. Grease 12 muffin cups with cooking spray. Fill cups 3/4 full. Preheat barbecue to high. Place muffin pan on 1 side of ungreased grill. Turn off burner under muffin pan, turning opposite burner down to medium. Close lid. Cook for about 25 minutes, rotating pan at halftime, until muffins are golden and wooden pick inserted in centre of muffin comes out clean. Let stand in pan for 5 minutes before removing to wire rack to cool. Makes 12 muffins.

1 muffin: 157 Calories; 5 g Total Fat (2.9 g Mono, 0.6 g Poly, 1.1 g Sat); 19 mg Cholesterol; 25 g Carbohydrate; 1 g Fibre; 4 g Protein; 287 mg Sodium

Pictured on page 31.

Photo Legend, next page

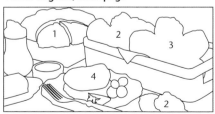

1. Barbecued Biscuit, page 32
2. Corn Muffins, page 28
3. Blueberry Muffins, above
4. Buttermilk Pancakes, page 33

Hot biscuits are a great addition to any meal.

note

To make sour milk, measure 1 tbsp. (15 mL) white vinegar or lemon juice into 1 cup (250 mL) liquid measure. Add milk to make 3/4 cup (175 mL) liquid. Stir.

serving suggestion

An ideal side for Chicken And Artichoke Salad, page 38, or Barbecued Pork Salad, page 45.

Barbecued Biscuit

All-purpose flour	2 cups	500 mL
Baking powder	4 tsp.	20 mL
Baking soda	1/2 tsp.	2 mL
Salt	3/4 tsp.	4 mL
Hard margarine (or butter), cut up	3 tbsp.	50 mL
Sour milk (see Note)	3/4 cup	175 mL

Combine first 4 ingredients in medium bowl. Cut in margarine until mixture resembles coarse crumbs.

Add sour milk. Stir until just moistened. Turn out dough onto lightly floured surface. Knead 8 to 10 times. Flatten dough into 3/4 inch (2 cm) thick disc. Place on 1 sheet of greased heavy-duty (or double layer of regular) foil. Do not enclose. Preheat barbecue to high. Place foil with dough on 1 side of ungreased grill. Turn off burner under foil, turning opposite burner down to medium. Close lid. Cook for 15 to 18 minutes, rotating foil at halftime, until biscuit is lightly golden. Cuts into 8 wedges.

1 wedge: 170 Calories; 4.9 g Total Fat (2.9 g Mono, 0.6 g Poly, 1.1 g Sat); 1 mg Cholesterol; 27 g Carbohydrate; 1 g Fibre; 4 g Protein; 551 mg Sodium

Pictured on page 30.

Buttermilk Pancakes

All-purpose flour	2 cups	500 mL
Baking powder	2 tsp.	10 mL
Baking soda	1 tsp.	5 mL
Salt	1 tsp.	5 mL
Buttermilk (or reconstituted from powder)	2 cups	500 mL
Cooking oil	2 tbsp.	30 mL
Large eggs	2	2
Cooking oil	2 tsp.	10 mL

Measure first 4 ingredients into large bowl. Stir. Make a well in centre.

Combine next 3 ingredients in medium bowl. Add to well. Stir until just moistened. Batter will be lumpy.

Place griddle on barbecue grill. Preheat barbecue to medium. Brush 1/2 tsp. (2 mL) of second amount of cooking oil on griddle. Heat until hot. Pour about 1/4 cup (60 mL) batter onto griddle for each pancake. Cook for 2 to 3 minutes until edges of pancakes appear dry and bubbles form on top. Turn. Cook for about 2 minutes until golden. Repeat with remaining batter, brushing more cooking oil on griddle with each batch if necessary to prevent sticking. Makes 14 pancakes.

1 pancake: 118 Calories; 3.9 g Total Fat (1.9 g Mono, 1 g Poly, 0.6 g Sat); 32 mg Cholesterol; 16 g Carbohydrate; 1 g Fibre; 4 g Protein; 362 mg Sodium

Pictured on page 30.

Put the griddle on the barbecue and enjoy an outdoor brunch. Don't have a griddle? A cast-iron frying pan works just as well.

serving suggestion

Add an assortment of fresh fruit on the side for a complete breakfast.

Crispy on the outside; tender and golden on the inside. Oregano and chili accent Cheddar cheese in this delicious bread.

Chili Herb Bread

Finely grated sharp Cheddar cheese	2/3 cup	150 mL
Hard margarine (or butter), softened	2/3 cup	150 mL
Chili powder	1 tsp.	5 mL
Dried whole oregano	3/4 tsp.	4 mL
French bread loaf, cut into 1 inch (2.5 cm) thick slices	1	1

Measure first 4 ingredients into small bowl. Beat well. Makes about 1 1/4 cups (300 mL) cheese mixture.

Spread cheese mixture evenly on 1 side of each bread slice. Arrange slices into loaf shape. Place on 1 sheet of heavy-duty (or double layer of regular) foil. Fold edges of foil to enclose. Preheat barbecue to medium. Place foil with loaf on ungreased grill. Close lid. Cook for about 15 minutes, turning occasionally, until cheese is melted. Makes about 14 slices.

1 slice: 195 Calories; 12.1 g Total Fat (6.9 g Mono, 1.2 g Poly, 3.3 g Sat); 6 mg Cholesterol; 17 g Carbohydrate; 1 g Fibre; 4 g Protein; 343 mg Sodium

Pictured on page 35.

Don't discard the drippings from your barbecued roast. Use them in this delicious recipe. Cook the Yorkshire pudding on the barbecue before slicing the roast.

Yorkshire Pudding

All-purpose flour	1 cup	250 mL
Milk	1 cup	250 mL
Large eggs	2	2
Salt	1/2 tsp.	2 mL
Cooking oil (or roast beef drippings)	2 tbsp.	30 mL

Beat first 4 ingredients in small bowl until smooth.

Spread cooking oil evenly in 9 x 9 inch (22 x 22 cm) shallow pan. Preheat barbecue to high. Place pan on 1 side of ungreased grill. Turn off burner under pan, turning opposite burner down to medium-high. Heat cooking oil until hot. Pour batter into pan. Spread evenly. Close lid. Cook for about 30 minutes, rotating pan at halftime, until lightly golden. Cuts into 9 pieces.

1 piece: 109 Calories; 4.6 g Total Fat (2.3 g Mono, 1.1 g Poly, 0.8 g Sat); 49 mg Cholesterol; 13 g Carbohydrate; trace Fibre; 4 g Protein; 160 mg Sodium

Pictured on page 35.

Top: Chili Herb Bread, above
Bottom: Yorkshire Pudding, above

Fresh, grilled vegetables are tossed with a flavourful pesto in this appetizing salad your guests will love.

Grilled Pesto Vegetable Salad

Green medium peppers, quartered, seeds and ribs removed	2	2
Red medium peppers, quartered, seeds and ribs removed	2	2
Medium zucchini (with peel), cut lengthwise into 1/4 inch (6 mm) thick slices	3	3
Red medium onions, each cut into 8 wedges	2	2
SPINACH PESTO		
Fresh spinach, stems removed, lightly packed	1 cup	250 mL
Pine nuts, toasted (see Note)	1/4 cup	60 mL
Grated Parmesan cheese	1/4 cup	60 mL
Olive (or cooking) oil	1/4 cup	60 mL
Balsamic vinegar	1 tbsp.	15 mL
Granulated sugar	1 tsp.	5 mL
Salt	1/4 tsp.	1 mL

Preheat barbecue to high. Arrange green and red peppers, skin-side down, on greased grill. Cook for 10 to 15 minutes until skins are blistered and blackened. Remove to medium bowl. Cover with plastic wrap. Let sweat for about 15 minutes until cool enough to handle. Peel and discard skins. Cut into 1/2 inch (12 mm) wide slices. Transfer to large bowl.

Cook zucchini and onion on greased grill for 3 to 5 minutes per side until tender-crisp and grill marks appear. Add to pepper. Toss gently.

Spinach Pesto: Process all 7 ingredients in blender or food processor until smooth. Makes about 2/3 cup (150 mL) pesto. Spoon over pepper mixture. Toss. Makes about 6 cups (1.5 L) salad. Serves 4.

1 serving: 304 Calories; 22.4 g Total Fat (13.3 g Mono, 3.8 g Poly, 4.2 g Sat); 5 mg Cholesterol; 23 g Carbohydrate; 7 g Fibre; 9 g Protein; 293 mg Sodium

Pictured on page 37.

A colourful, tangy salad that's perfect for company.

note

To toast nuts, spread evenly in ungreased shallow pan. Bake in 350°F (175°C) oven for 5 to 10 minutes, stirring or shaking often, until desired doneness.

Chicken And Artichoke Salad

BALSAMIC MARINADE

Olive (or cooking) oil	1/3 cup	75 mL
Balsamic vinegar	1/4 cup	60 mL
Liquid honey	2 tbsp.	30 mL
Chopped fresh basil (or 3/4 tsp., 4 mL, dried)	1 tbsp.	15 mL
Garlic cloves, minced (or 1/2 tsp., 2 mL, powder)	2	2
Lemon pepper	1 tsp.	5 mL
Boneless, skinless chicken breast halves	3/4 lb.	340 g
Large red onion, cut into 8 wedges	1	1
Bag of fresh spinach (about 3 1/2 cups, 875 mL, stems removed, lightly packed)	6 oz.	170 g
Can of artichoke hearts, drained and coarsely chopped	14 oz.	398 mL
Halved cherry tomatoes	1 cup	250 mL
Chopped walnuts, toasted (see Note)	1 cup	250 mL
Crumbled feta cheese (about 4 oz., 113 g)	3/4 cup	175 mL

Balsamic Marinade: Combine first 6 ingredients in jar with tight-fitting lid. Shake well. Makes about 3/4 cup (175 mL) marinade.

Place chicken in large resealable freezer bag. Pour 1/2 of marinade over top. Seal bag. Turn until coated. Marinate in refrigerator for 3 hours. Drain and discard marinade. Preheat barbecue to medium. Cook chicken on greased grill for about 5 minutes per side until no longer pink inside. Chop coarsely. Transfer to large bowl.

Cook onion on greased grill for about 10 minutes, turning once, until softened and grill marks appear. Add to chicken.

Add remaining 5 ingredients. Toss. Drizzle with remaining marinade. Toss. Makes about 11 cups (2.75 L) salad. Serves 6.

1 serving: 369 Calories; 24.4 g Total Fat (8.7 g Mono, 9.3 g Poly, 4.9 g Sat); 58 mg Cholesterol; 15 g Carbohydrate; 4 g Fibre; 26 g Protein; 459 mg Sodium

Pictured on page 39.

The dramatic colours of this salad are unique and visually striking. The lively citrus flavour will awaken your taste buds.

note

To toast nuts, spread evenly in ungreased shallow pan. Bake in 350°F (175°C) oven for 5 to 10 minutes, stirring or shaking often, until desired doneness.

Fennel And Sausage Salad

ORANGE DRESSING

Olive (or cooking) oil	1/2 cup	125 mL
Red wine vinegar	1/4 cup	60 mL
Orange juice	1/4 cup	60 mL
Garlic clove, minced (or 1/4 tsp., 1 mL, powder)	1	1
Salt	1/4 tsp.	1 mL
Pepper, just a pinch		
Sultana raisins	1/2 cup	125 mL
Thick pork sausages (about 12 oz., 340 g)	4	4
Medium oranges, peeled and segmented	2 – 3	2 – 3
Head of radicchio, chopped or torn	1	1
Fennel bulb (white part only), thinly sliced	1	1
Pine nuts, toasted (see Note)	1/2 cup	125 mL

Orange Dressing: Combine first 6 ingredients in jar with tight-fitting lid. Shake well. Makes about 1 cup (250 mL) dressing.

Measure raisins into small bowl. Add 1/2 of dressing. Stir. Cover. Let stand for 30 minutes.

Preheat barbecue to medium. Cook sausages on greased grill for about 20 minutes, turning occasionally, until no longer pink inside. Cut diagonally into 1 inch (2.5 cm) pieces. Transfer to large bowl.

Add raisin mixture and remaining 4 ingredients. Toss. Drizzle with remaining dressing. Toss. Makes about 10 cups (2.5 L) salad. Serves 6.

1 serving: 538 Calories; 43.4 g Total Fat (24.6 g Mono, 6.8 g Poly, 9.7 g Sat); 51 mg Cholesterol; 24 g Carbohydrate; 3 g Fibre; 18 g Protein; 736 mg Sodium

Pictured on page 43.

Mango Beef Salad

Lemon pepper	1 tbsp.	15 mL
Olive (or cooking) oil	2 tsp.	10 mL
Garlic clove, minced (or 1/4 tsp., 1 mL, powder)	1	1
Boneless strip loin steaks (about 10 oz., 285 g, each)	2	2
Mixed salad greens, lightly packed	5 cups	1.25 L
Can of sliced mango with syrup, drained and coarsely chopped	14 oz.	398 mL
Cashews, toasted (see Note) and coarsely chopped	1/2 cup	125 mL
Bacon slices, cooked crisp and crumbled	8	8
MAPLE DRESSING		
Peanut (or cooking) oil	1/3 cup	75 mL
Red wine vinegar	2 tbsp.	30 mL
Maple (or maple-flavoured) syrup	2 tbsp.	30 mL
Soy sauce	2 tsp.	10 mL
Salt	1/4 tsp.	1 mL

Combine first 3 ingredients in small bowl.

Divide and spread evenly on both sides of each steak. Preheat barbecue to medium-high. Cook steaks on greased grill for about 5 minutes per side until desired doneness. Let stand for 10 minutes. Slice into 1/8 inch (3 mm) thick slices. Transfer to large bowl.

Add next 4 ingredients. Toss gently.

Maple Dressing: Combine all 5 ingredients in jar with tight-fitting lid. Shake well. Makes about 2/3 cup (150 mL) dressing. Pour over steak mixture. Toss gently. Makes about 11 cups (2.75 L) salad. Serves 8.

1 serving: 313 Calories; 22.7 g Total Fat (11.2 g Mono, 4.4 g Poly, 5.6 g Sat); 37 mg Cholesterol; 12 g Carbohydrate; 1 g Fibre; 16 g Protein; 740 mg Sodium

Pictured on page 43.

Smoky bacon is a nice addition to tangy mangoes, crisp vegetables and juicy steak. This will become a favourite!

note

To toast nuts, spread evenly in ungreased shallow pan. Bake in 350°F (175°C) oven for 5 to 10 minutes, stirring or shaking often, until desired doneness.

Photo Legend, next page

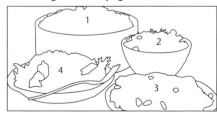

1. Veggie Pasta Salad, page 44
2. Mango Beef Salad, above
3. Fennel And Sausage Salad, page 40
4. Barbecued Pork Salad, page 45

Grilled vegetables tossed with pasta in a creamy sun-dried tomato sauce. Delicious!

Veggie Pasta Salad

Roma (plum) tomatoes, cut into wedges	8	8
Chopped green onion	1/2 cup	125 mL
Olive (or cooking) oil	2 tbsp.	30 mL
Balsamic vinegar	2 tbsp.	30 mL
Garlic clove, minced (or 1/4 tsp., 1 mL, powder)	1	1
Italian no-salt seasoning (such as Mrs. Dash)	1/2 tsp.	2 mL
Granulated sugar	1/2 tsp.	2 mL
Salt, sprinkle		
Pepper, sprinkle		
Large red peppers, quartered, seeds and ribs removed	2	2
Medium zucchini (with peel), cut lengthwise into 1/4 inch (6 mm) thick slices	2	2
Eggplant (with peel), cut lengthwise into 1/4 inch (6 mm) thick slices	1	1
Cooked penne pasta (about 2 cups, 500 mL, uncooked), chilled	4 cups	1 L
Sour cream	1/3 cup	75 mL
Sun-dried tomato pesto	1/4 cup	60 mL

Put first 9 ingredients into medium bowl. Stir. Transfer to greased 8 × 8 inch (20 × 20 cm) foil pan. Preheat barbecue to medium-high. Place pan on ungreased grill. Close lid. Cook for about 15 minutes, stirring occasionally, until tomato is softened. Transfer tomato mixture with slotted spoon to large bowl. Discard liquid.

Cook red peppers on greased grill for about 15 minutes, turning occasionally, until grill marks appear and skins are slightly blackened. Chop coarsely. Add to tomato mixture.

Cook zucchini and eggplant slices on greased grill for 3 to 4 minutes per side until softened and grill marks appear. Chop coarsely. Add to tomato mixture. Add pasta. Toss gently.

Combine sour cream and pesto in small bowl. Add to pasta mixture. Toss gently. Makes about 10 cups (2.5 L) salad. Serves 6.

1 serving: 292 Calories; 8.1 g Total Fat (4.1 g Mono, 1.1 g Poly, 2 g Sat); 5 mg Cholesterol; 50 g Carbohydrate; 7 g Fibre; 9 g Protein; 79 mg Sodium

Pictured on pages 42/43.

Barbecued Pork Salad

Small oranges, peeled and white pith removed, thinly sliced	4	4
Thinly sliced red onion	2/3 cup	150 mL
ORANGE DRESSING		
Olive (or cooking) oil	1/3 cup	75 mL
Orange juice	1/4 cup	60 mL
Apple cider vinegar	3 tbsp.	50 mL
Liquid honey	1 tbsp.	15 mL
Grated orange zest	1/2 tsp.	2 mL
Dried basil	1/2 tsp.	2 mL
Garlic powder	1/8 tsp.	0.5 mL
Salt	1/4 tsp.	1 mL
Pepper, sprinkle		
Pork tenderloin, trimmed of fat	1 lb.	454 g
Garlic and herb no-salt seasoning (such as Mrs. Dash)	1 tsp.	5 mL
Pepper, sprinkle		
Mixed salad greens, lightly packed	10 cups	2.5 L

Place orange slices and onion in large bowl. Toss gently.

Orange Dressing: Process first 9 ingredients in blender or food processor until smooth. Makes about 1 cup (250 mL) dressing. Pour over orange mixture. Toss gently. Cover. Chill for 2 hours.

Cut tenderloin almost in half lengthwise, but not quite through to other side. Press open to flatten. Sprinkle both sides with seasoning and pepper. Preheat barbecue to medium. Place tenderloin on greased grill. Close lid. Cook for 15 to 20 minutes, turning once, until meat thermometer inserted into thickest part of tenderloin reads 155°F (68°C). Remove from heat. Cover with foil. Let stand for 10 minutes. Internal temperature should rise to at least 160°F (70°C).

Add salad greens to orange mixture. Toss gently. Divide among 4 individual salad plates. Cut tenderloin into 1/4 inch (6 mm) thick slices. Arrange 4 to 5 slices of pork on top of each salad. Serves 4.

1 serving: 423 Calories; 24.3 g Total Fat (16.1 g Mono, 2.2 g Poly, 4.2 g Sat); 66 mg Cholesterol; 28 g Carbohydrate; 5 g Fibre; 26 g Protein; 222 mg Sodium

Spiced strips of pork and tangy orange dressing make salad greens delightful. Serve with crusty bread—yum!

Pictured on page 42.

If you have travelled to Australia, you may have already experienced these hamburgers-with-the-works. Stacked high with sliced beets, bacon, egg, cheese, onions and more, this is a meal-in-a-bun!

Super Oz Burgers

Cooking oil	1 tbsp.	15 mL
Medium onions, thinly sliced	3	3
Large eggs (optional)	6	6
Finely chopped onion	3/4 cup	175 mL
Fresh bread crumbs	1/3 cup	75 mL
Large egg, fork-beaten	1	1
Barbecue sauce	2 tbsp.	30 mL
Salt	1/4 tsp.	1 mL
Pepper	1/4 tsp.	1 mL
Lean ground beef	1 lb.	454 g
Hamburger buns, split	6	6
Barbecue sauce	1/3 cup	75 mL
Can of sliced beets (12 – 18 slices)	14 oz.	398 mL
Cheddar cheese slices	6	6
Medium tomatoes, sliced	2	2
Bacon slices, cooked almost crisp	6	6
Green leaf lettuce leaves	6	6

Preheat barbecue to medium. Heat cooking oil on griddle or in large cast-iron pan on barbecue. Add onion. Cook for 5 to 10 minutes, stirring often, until softened. Remove onion to medium bowl. Cover to keep warm.

Reduce heat to medium-low. Break 3 eggs onto same griddle. When eggs start to set, add about 1 tbsp. (15 mL) water. Cover. Cook for about 1 minute until egg whites are set and yolks reach desired doneness, adding more water if needed. Remove eggs to plate. Cover to keep warm. Repeat with remaining 3 eggs.

Combine next 6 ingredients in large bowl. Add ground beef. Mix well. Divide and shape into 6 patties, about 5 inches (12.5 cm) in diameter. Increase heat to medium. Cook patties on greased grill for about 6 minutes per side until no longer pink inside.

Place buns, cut-side down, on greased grill. Toast until lightly browned.

Spread second amount of barbecue sauce on bottom half of each bun. Top each with patty, onion, beets, cheese, egg, tomato, bacon and lettuce. Cover with top half of each bun. Makes 6 burgers.

1 burger: 563 Calories; 30.6 g Total Fat (12.3 g Mono, 2.7 g Poly, 12.9 g Sat); 113 mg Cholesterol; 41 g Carbohydrate; 4 g Fibre; 31 g Protein; 1267 mg Sodium

Pictured on page 47.

The sweet taste of red peppers and honeyed pineapple sets this burger apart. Appealing in looks and taste.

make ahead

Burger patties can be made ahead using fresh lean ground beef (not previously frozen). Place patties in airtight container, with waxed paper between each layer. Store in freezer for up to 2 months.

Pineapple Pepper Burgers

Fresh bread crumbs	3/4 cup	175 mL
Finely chopped red pepper	3/4 cup	175 mL
Ketchup	1/3 cup	75 mL
Finely chopped onion	1/4 cup	60 mL
Sweet (or regular) chili sauce	2 tbsp.	30 mL
Chopped fresh cilantro or parsley (or 1 1/2 tsp., 7 mL, dried)	2 tbsp.	30 mL
Large egg	1	1
Salt	1 1/2 tsp.	7 mL
Pepper	1/4 tsp.	1 mL
Lean ground beef	1 1/2 lbs.	680 g
Pineapple slices	6	6
Soy sauce	2 tbsp.	30 mL
Liquid honey	1 tbsp.	15 mL
Kaiser buns, split	6	6
Red leaf lettuce leaves	6	6

Combine first 9 ingredients in large bowl.

Add ground beef. Mix well. Divide and shape into 6 patties, about 4 inches (10 cm) in diameter. Preheat barbecue to medium. Cook patties on greased grill for about 6 minutes per side until no longer pink inside.

Blot pineapple slices with paper towel. Combine soy sauce and honey in small bowl. Brush soy sauce mixture over both sides of each pineapple slice. Cook pineapple slices on greased grill for 2 to 3 minutes per side until grill marks appear.

Place buns, cut-side down, on greased grill. Toast until lightly browned. Place 1 lettuce leaf on bottom half of each bun. Top each with patty and pineapple slice. Cover with top half of each bun. Makes 6 burgers.

1 burger: *545 Calories; 21.3 g Total Fat (8.7 g Mono, 2.1 g Poly, 7.6 g Sat); 100 mg Cholesterol; 56 g Carbohydrate; 2 g Fibre; 31 g Protein; 1706 mg Sodium*

Pictured on page 51 and back cover.

Salmon Burgers

Peanut (or cooking) oil	1 tbsp.	15 mL
Medium onions, thinly sliced	2	2
Salt	1/8 tsp.	0.5 mL
Pepper	1/8 tsp.	0.5 mL
Salmon fillets, skin and bones removed, cut into 8 equal pieces (see Note)	2 lbs.	900 g
Peanut (or cooking) oil	1 tbsp.	15 mL
Lemon pepper	2 tbsp.	30 mL
Buns (your choice), split	8	8
Sour cream	1/2 cup	125 mL
Sweet (or regular) chili sauce	3 tbsp.	50 mL
Medium tomatoes, sliced	2	2

Preheat barbecue to medium-low. Heat first amount of peanut oil on griddle or in large cast-iron pan on barbecue. Add onion, salt and pepper. Cook for 5 to 10 minutes, stirring often, until onion is softened. Remove from heat. Keep warm.

Increase heat to medium. Brush salmon pieces with second amount of peanut oil. Sprinkle with lemon pepper. Cook salmon on greased grill for about 5 minutes per side, depending on thickness, until salmon flakes easily when tested with fork.

Place buns, cut-side down, on greased grill. Toast until lightly browned.

Combine sour cream and chili sauce in small bowl. Spread mixture on toasted sides of each bun.

Place 1 salmon piece on bottom half of each bun. Top each with onion mixture and tomato slices. Cover with top half of each bun. Makes 8 salmon burgers.

1 salmon burger: 410 Calories; 20.1 g Total Fat (7.7 g Mono, 6.1 g Poly, 4.9 g Sat); 72 mg Cholesterol; 29 g Carbohydrate; 1 g Fibre; 27 g Protein; 1333 mg Sodium

Pictured on page 50 and back cover.

Thick, grilled salmon burgers that are a bit messy to eat—but so good!

note

For even cooking, choose fillets from the thicker centre of the salmon, rather than from the thinner tail end.

Photo Legend, next page

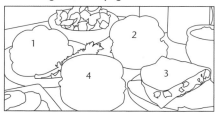

1. Salmon Burgers, this page
2. Pineapple Pepper Burgers, page 48
3. Grilled Quesadillas, page 52
4. Spicy Cheeseburgers, page 53

Crispy and golden on the outside with a spicy chicken filling on the inside.

Grilled Quesadillas

Sour cream	1/3 cup	75 mL
Chili sauce	2 tbsp.	30 mL
Chopped cooked chicken	3 cups	750 mL
Grated Monterey Jack cheese	1 2/3 cups	400 mL
Flour tortillas (10 inch, 25 cm, diameter)	4	4
Sliced pickled jalapeño peppers	1 – 2 tbsp.	15 – 30 mL
Medium tomatoes, seeds removed, diced	2	2
Finely chopped green onion	3 tbsp.	50 mL
Chopped fresh parsley (or 1 1/2 tsp., 7 mL, flakes)	2 tbsp.	30 mL
Cooking oil	1 tbsp.	15 mL

Combine sour cream and chili sauce in medium bowl. Add chicken. Toss until coated.

Divide and scatter cheese over 1/2 of each tortilla. Divide and spoon chicken mixture evenly over cheese.

Layer next 4 ingredients over chicken mixture. Fold each tortilla in half to enclose filling.

Preheat barbecue to medium. Brush tops of folded tortillas with 1/2 of cooking oil. Cook quesadillas, top-side down, on greased grill for 5 minutes. Brush with remaining cooking oil. Turn. Cook for about 5 minutes until crisp and golden and cheese is melted. Cut in half to serve. Serves 4.

1 serving: 656 Calories; 33.7 g Total Fat (11.8 g Mono, 5 g Poly, 14.4 g Sat); 152 mg Cholesterol; 36 g Carbohydrate; 3 g Fibre; 51 g Protein; 772 mg Sodium

Pictured on page 51 and back cover.

Spicy Cheeseburgers

Fresh bread crumbs	1/4 cup	60 mL
Finely chopped red onion	1/4 cup	60 mL
Large egg, fork-beaten	1	1
Taco seasoning mix, stir before measuring	3 tbsp.	50 mL
Lime juice	2 tbsp.	30 mL
Chopped fresh oregano leaves (or 3/4 tsp., 4 mL, dried)	1 tbsp.	15 mL
Pepper, sprinkle		
Lean ground beef	1 lb.	454 g
Cheddar cheese slices	4	4
Hamburger buns, split	4	4
Sour cream	1/4 cup	60 mL
Medium tomato, thinly sliced	1	1
Salsa	1/4 cup	60 mL

Combine first 7 ingredients in medium bowl.

Add ground beef. Mix well. Divide and shape into 8 thin patties, about 5 inches (12.5 cm) in diameter.

Place 1 cheese slice on each of 4 patties. Top with remaining 4 patties. Pinch patty edges to enclose cheese. Preheat barbecue to medium-high. Cook patties on greased grill for about 6 minutes per side until no longer pink inside.

Place buns, cut-side down, on greased grill. Toast until lightly browned.

Place 1 patty on bottom half of each bun. Dollop each with 1 tbsp. (15 mL) sour cream. Top each with tomato slices and 1 tbsp. (15 mL) salsa. Cover with top half of each bun. Makes 4 cheeseburgers.

1 cheeseburger: 594 Calories; 33.4 g Total Fat (12.5 g Mono, 1.9 g Poly, 15.3 g Sat); 153 mg Cholesterol; 37 g Carbohydrate; 2 g Fibre; 36 g Protein; 1881 mg Sodium

Pictured on pages 50/51 and back cover.

Taco seasoning and the tang of lime make these burgers Tex-Mex. The cheesy surprise inside will have everyone asking for seconds.

make ahead

Burger patties can be made ahead using fresh lean ground beef (not previously frozen). Place patties in airtight container, with waxed paper between each layer. Store in freezer for up to 2 months.

Tender, moist chicken with a hint of lime and just the right amount of spices to make it memorable.

variation

Brush wraps with 1 tbsp. (15 mL) cooking oil. Cook wraps on greased grill on medium for 5 to 7 minutes, turning occasionally, until crisp and golden.

Chicken Wraps

Chopped fresh cilantro or parsley (or 1 tbsp., 15 mL, dried)	1/4 cup	60 mL
Cooking oil	3 tbsp.	50 mL
Dried crushed chilies (optional)	2 tsp.	10 mL
Ground cumin	1 tsp.	5 mL
Garlic cloves, minced (or 1/2 tsp., 2 mL, powder)	2	2
Boneless, skinless chicken breast halves	1 lb.	454 g
Lime juice	1/4 cup	60 mL
Corn relish	1/4 cup	60 mL
Sour cream	1/4 cup	60 mL
Flour tortillas (10 inch, 25 cm, diameter)	4	4
Large ripe avocado, sliced	1	1
Red medium pepper, seeds and ribs removed, thinly sliced	1	1
Grated medium Cheddar cheese	1 cup	250 mL

Combine first 5 ingredients in medium bowl.

Add chicken. Stir. Cover with plastic wrap. Chill for at least 1 hour, stirring occasionally.

Add lime juice to chicken mixture. Stir. Drain and discard liquid. Preheat barbecue to medium. Cook chicken on greased grill for about 5 minutes per side until no longer pink inside. Cut diagonally into thin slices. Cover to keep warm.

Measure corn relish and sour cream into small bowl. Stir. Spread about 2 tbsp. (30 mL) on each tortilla.

Divide and layer chicken, avocado, red pepper and cheese across centre of each tortilla, leaving 2 inches (5 cm) at each side. Fold sides over filling. Roll up from bottom to enclose filling. Slice in half diagonally. Serves 8.

1 serving: 337 Calories; 18.3 g Total Fat (8.2 g Mono, 3.3 g Poly, 5.4 g Sat); 59 mg Cholesterol; 21 g Carbohydrate; 2 g Fibre; 23 g Protein; 252 mg Sodium

Pictured on page 55.

Tasty grilled sandwiches to serve any time of the day! The sweet apple slices add crispness to the soft filling.

Apple And Cheese Grill

Hard margarine (or butter), softened	6 tbsp.	100 mL
Thick slices of raisin bread	8	8
Honey prepared mustard	1/4 cup	60 mL
Deli ham slices (about 6 oz., 170 g)	12	12
Large cooking apple (such as McIntosh), peeled and core removed, thinly sliced	1	1
Grated sharp Cheddar cheese	1 1/2 cups	375 mL

Spread margarine on 1 side of each bread slice. Place 4 bread slices, margarine-side down, on cutting board. Spread mustard on each.

Divide and layer ham slices, apple slices and cheese over each bread slice. Cover with remaining 4 bread slices, margarine-side up. Preheat barbecue to medium. Cook sandwiches on greased grill for about 6 minutes per side until golden and cheese is melted. Makes 4 sandwiches.

1 sandwich: 612 Calories; 39.4 g Total Fat (19.1 g Mono, 3.1 g Poly, 15.1 g Sat); 71 mg Cholesterol; 43 g Carbohydrate; 3 g Fibre; 23 g Protein; 1345 mg Sodium

Pictured on page 57.

Exotic flavours make this roast an impressive entrée. If the roast has excess fat, trim a piece off and use it to grease the grill.

note

To crack peppercorns, place whole peppercorns in small plastic bag. Tap peppercorns with heavy object, such as meat mallet or hammer, until cracked.

serving suggestion

Serve with grilled red onion wedges.

Sesame Pepper-Crusted Beef Roast

Rib-eye roast, trimmed of fat	3 lbs.	1.4 kg
Garlic cloves, halved	3	3
Olive (or cooking) oil	1 tbsp.	15 mL
Sesame seeds	1/4 cup	60 mL
Whole black peppercorns, cracked (see Note)	2 tbsp.	30 mL
Curry powder	2 tsp.	10 mL

Cut 6 shallow slits in roast at random. Insert garlic clove half into each slit. Brush olive oil over roast.

Combine remaining 3 ingredients in small bowl. Spread evenly on ungreased baking sheet. Roll roast in sesame seed mixture until coated. Preheat barbecue to medium-high. Place roast on 1 side of greased grill over drip pan. Turn off burner under roast, leaving opposite burner on medium-high. Close lid. Cook for 30 minutes. Reduce heat to medium. Cook for about 30 minutes until meat thermometer inserted into centre of roast reads 135°F (57°C) for rare to 165°F (74°C) for well done. Remove from heat. Cover with foil. Let stand for 10 minutes. Cut into 1/2 inch (12 mm) slices. Makes 12 servings (2 to 3 oz., 57 to 85 g each, cooked weight).

1 serving: 208 Calories; 10.4 g Total Fat (4.7 g Mono, 1.1 g Poly, 3.4 g Sat); 55 mg Cholesterol; 2 g Carbohydrate; 1 g Fibre; 25 g Protein; 72 mg Sodium

Pictured on page 59.

The most tender and juicy beef of all. Sure to please.

Grilled Beef Tenderloin

Hard margarine (or butter), melted	1/4 cup	60 mL
Red wine vinegar	1/2 tbsp.	7 mL
Worcestershire sauce	1 tsp.	5 mL
Beef bouillon powder	1/2 tsp.	2 mL
Beef tenderloin roast	2 1/4 lbs.	1 kg

Combine first 4 ingredients in small bowl.

Brush roast with margarine mixture. Preheat barbecue to high. Sear all sides of roast on greased grill. Reduce heat to medium-high. Move roast on 1 side of grill over drip pan. Turn off burner under roast, leaving opposite burner on medium-high. Close lid. Cook for about 60 minutes, turning occasionally and brushing with margarine mixture, until meat thermometer inserted into thickest part of roast reads 160°F (70°C) for medium, or until desired doneness. Cut into 1/2 inch (12 mm) slices. Makes 9 servings (2 to 3 oz., 57 to 85 g each, cooked weight).

1 serving: 178 Calories; 11 g Total Fat (5.6 g Mono, 0.8 g Poly, 3.2 g Sat); 44 mg Cholesterol; 0 g Carbohydrate; 0 g Fibre; 18 g Protein; 144 mg Sodium

Pictured on page 61.

A spicy steak that tastes great either warm or cold.

serving suggestion

Try it in a fajita or with diced peppers tossed with rice.

Spanish Sirloin

Paprika	2 tbsp.	30 mL
Lemon juice	2 tbsp.	30 mL
Garlic cloves, minced (or 1 tsp., 5 mL, powder)	4	4
Pepper	1 tsp.	5 mL
Beef sirloin tip steak	2 lbs.	900 g

Combine first 4 ingredients in small bowl.

Spread paprika mixture on both sides of steak. Preheat barbecue to medium. Cook steak on greased grill for 7 to 10 minutes per side until desired doneness. Remove from heat. Cover with foil. Let stand for 10 minutes. Cut into 1/4 inch (6 mm) thick slices. Makes 8 servings (2 to 3 oz., 57 to 85 g each, cooked weight).

1 serving: 154 Calories; 7.5 g Total Fat (3.2 g Mono, 0.4 g Poly, 2.9 g Sat); 49 mg Cholesterol; 2 g Carbohydrate; trace Fibre; 19 g Protein; 36 mg Sodium

Pictured on page 61.

Top: Grilled Beef Tenderloin, above
Bottom: Spanish Sirloin, above

Crisp, fresh vegetables and deliciously barbecued steak—what a combination! Vegetables may need to be cooked in two batches.

Grilled Steak And Vegetables

BARBECUED VEGETABLES

Fresh whole white mushrooms	18 – 20	18 – 20
Medium zucchini (with peel), cut into 1/2 inch (12 mm) thick slices	2	2
Red medium onion, cut into wedges	1	1
Red medium pepper, cut into wedges, seeds and ribs removed	1	1
Yellow medium pepper, cut into wedges, seeds and ribs removed	1	1
Low-fat Italian dressing	3/4 cup	175 mL
Brown sugar, packed	2 tbsp.	30 mL
Olive (or cooking) oil	1 tbsp.	15 mL
Dry mustard	1 tsp.	5 mL
Ground coriander	1 tsp.	5 mL
Garlic cloves, minced (or 3/4 tsp., 4 mL, powder)	3	3
Salt	1 tsp.	5 mL
Pepper	2 tsp.	10 mL
Top sirloin, flank or inside round steak	2 lbs.	900 g

Barbecued Vegetables: Put first 5 ingredients into large bowl. Add dressing. Stir until coated. Cover with plastic wrap. Marinate in refrigerator for 2 to 3 hours, stirring occasionally. Drain and discard liquid from vegetables. Spread vegetable mixture evenly in large greased foil pan. Preheat barbecue to medium. Place pan on ungreased grill. Cook vegetables for 8 to 10 minutes, stirring occasionally, until tender-crisp. Remove from heat. Cover with foil to keep warm.

Combine next 7 ingredients in small bowl.

Spread brown sugar mixture over both sides of steak. Reduce heat to medium-low. Cook steak on greased grill for 7 to 10 minutes per side until desired doneness. Cut diagonally into 1/4 inch (6 mm) thick slices. Serve with vegetables. Makes 8 servings (2 to 3 oz., 57 to 85 g each, cooked weight).

1 serving: 217 Calories; 9.9 g Total Fat (4.7 g Mono, 0.7 g Poly, 3.2 g Sat); 50 mg Cholesterol; 12 g Carbohydrate; 2 g Fibre; 21 g Protein; 505 mg Sodium

Pictured on page 63.

Full-bodied marinade and tasty vegetables make these delicious. Marinate overnight for even more flavour if desired.

serving suggestion

Serve with rice or Potatoes On A Stick, page 108.

Barbecued Kabobs

SWEET SOY MARINADE

Soy sauce	1/3 cup	75 mL
Granulated sugar	2 tbsp.	30 mL
Cooking oil	2 tbsp.	30 mL
Worcestershire sauce	1 tbsp.	15 mL
Garlic clove, minced (or 1/4 tsp., 2 mL, powder)	1	1
Red wine vinegar	1 1/2 tbsp.	25 mL
Pepper	1/8 tsp.	0.5 mL
Beef top sirloin steak, cut into sixteen 1 inch (2.5 cm) cubes	1 1/4 lbs.	560 g
Fresh whole white mushrooms	8	8
Red medium onion, cut into 8 wedges	1	1
Green medium pepper, seeds and ribs removed, cut into 1 inch (2.5 cm) pieces	1	1
Red medium pepper, seeds and ribs removed, cut into 1 inch (2.5 cm) pieces	1	1
Cherry tomatoes	8	8
Small zucchini (with peel), halved lengthwise, each half cut into 8 pieces	1	1
Bamboo skewers (8 inch, 20 cm, length), soaked in water for 10 minutes	8	8

Sweet Soy Marinade: Combine first 7 ingredients in large bowl. Makes about 1/2 cup (125 mL) marinade.

Add beef. Stir until coated. Cover with plastic wrap. Marinate in refrigerator for 30 minutes, stirring occasionally. Drain, reserving marinade in small saucepan. Bring reserved marinade to a boil on medium. Reduce heat to medium-low. Simmer, uncovered, for at least 5 minutes.

Thread beef and vegetables alternately onto skewers. Preheat barbecue to medium-high. Cook kabobs on greased grill for about 20 minutes, turning occasionally and brushing with reserved marinade, until desired doneness. Makes 8 kabobs.

1 kabob: 167 Calories; 8.2 g Total Fat (4 g Mono, 1.3 g Poly, 2.1 g Sat); 31 mg Cholesterol; 10 g Carbohydrate; 1 g Fibre; 14 g Protein; 771 mg Sodium

Pictured on page 65.

When rib lovers crave meaty, sticky ribs, these are the kind they're thinking about. Add a chopped fresh chili pepper or two if you can stand the heat.

Teriyaki Ribs

Beef ribs, whole slab	5 1/2 lbs.	2.7 kg
Teriyaki sauce	1/2 cup	125 mL
Liquid honey	1/2 cup	125 mL
Dijon mustard (with whole seeds)	1/3 cup	75 mL
Worcestershire sauce	1/4 cup	60 mL
Hot pepper sauce	1 tbsp.	15 mL
Garlic cloves, minced (or 1 tsp., 5 mL, powder)	4	4

Place ribs in shallow baking dish.

Combine remaining 6 ingredients in small bowl. Makes about 1 1/2 cups (375 mL) marinade. Pour over ribs. Turn until coated. Cover with plastic wrap. Marinate in refrigerator for at least 6 hours or overnight, turning occasionally. Drain, reserving marinade in small saucepan. Bring reserved marinade to a boil on medium. Reduce heat to medium-low. Simmer, uncovered, for at least 5 minutes. Preheat barbecue to medium-low. Place ribs on 1 side of greased grill over drip pan. Turn off burner under ribs, leaving opposite burner on medium-low. Close lid. Cook for about 1 1/2 hours, turning occasionally and brushing with reserved marinade, until tender. Serves 8.

1 serving: 390 Calories; 16.8 g Total Fat (7.2 g Mono, 0.9 g Poly, 7 g Sat); 77 mg Cholesterol; 27 g Carbohydrate; trace Fibre; 33 g Protein; 1074 mg Sodium

Pictured on divider.

Spicy, thick tomato marinade flavours this tender beef. Allow plenty of time to marinate.

Savoury Short Ribs

TOMATO MARINADE

Can of tomato sauce	7 1/2 oz.	213 mL
Apple cider vinegar	1/2 cup	125 mL
Cooking oil	1/4 cup	60 mL
Granulated sugar	1 1/2 tbsp.	25 mL
Dry onion flakes	1 tbsp.	15 mL
Worcestershire sauce	2 tsp.	10 mL
Prepared mustard	1 tsp.	5 mL
Chili powder	1 tsp.	5 mL
Pepper	1/2 tsp.	2 mL
Garlic powder	1/4 tsp.	1 mL

(continued on next page)

| Beef short ribs, bone-in | 3 lbs. | 1.4 kg |

Tomato Marinade: Combine first 10 ingredients in small bowl. Makes about 1 3/4 cups (425 mL) marinade.

Place short ribs in shallow baking dish. Pour marinade over ribs. Turn until coated. Cover with plastic wrap. Marinate in refrigerator for at least 6 hours or overnight, turning occasionally. Drain, reserving marinade in small saucepan. Bring reserved marinade to a boil on medium. Reduce heat to medium-low. Simmer, uncovered, for at least 5 minutes. Let ribs stand until room temperature before cooking. Preheat barbecue to low. Place ribs on greased grill. Close lid. Cook for about 45 minutes, turning occasionally and brushing with reserved marinade, until tender. Serves 4.

1 serving: 480 Calories; 32.4 g Total Fat (16.3 g Mono, 4.9 g Poly, 8.6 g Sat); 84 mg Cholesterol; 13 g Carbohydrate; 1 g Fibre; 35 g Protein; 455 mg Sodium

Pictured below.

Visible mustard seeds make this steak pleasing to look at, as well as delicious.

Mustard Seasoned Steak

MUSTARD WINE MARINADE

Dijon mustard (with whole seeds)	1/4 cup	60 mL
Dry white (or alcohol-free) wine	1/4 cup	60 mL
Apple cider vinegar	2 tbsp.	30 mL
Cooking oil	2 tbsp.	30 mL
Finely chopped fresh rosemary (or 3/4 tsp., 4 mL, dried, crushed)	1 tbsp.	15 mL
Pepper, sprinkle		
Flank steak	1 1/2 lbs.	680 g

Mustard Wine Marinade: Combine first 6 ingredients in small bowl. Makes about 2/3 cup (150 mL) marinade.

Put steak into large resealable freezer bag. Pour marinade over top. Seal bag. Turn until coated. Marinate in refrigerator for at least 6 hours or overnight, turning occasionally. Drain, reserving marinade in small saucepan. Bring reserved marinade to a boil on medium. Reduce heat to medium-low. Simmer, uncovered, for at least 5 minutes. Preheat barbecue to high. Cook steak on greased grill for 5 to 7 minutes per side, turning occasionally and brushing with reserved marinade, until desired doneness. Remove from heat. Cover with foil. Let stand for 10 minutes. Cut diagonally into very thin slices. Makes 6 servings (2 to 3 oz., 57 to 85 g each, cooked weight).

1 serving: 249 Calories; 14.1 g Total Fat (6.4 g Mono, 2.1 g Poly, 4.2 g Sat); 46 mg Cholesterol; 1 g Carbohydrate; 0 g Fibre; 27 g Protein; 198 mg Sodium

Pictured on page 69.

This tender and moist loaf tastes great hot off the barbecue.

Barbecued Meatloaf

Lean ground beef	1 1/2 lbs.	680 g
Finely chopped onion	1/3 cup	75 mL
Salt	1 1/2 tsp.	7 mL
Pepper	1/4 tsp.	1 mL
Chili sauce	1 cup	250 mL
Brown sugar, packed	1/4 cup	60 mL
White vinegar	2 tbsp.	30 mL
Dry mustard	1 tsp.	5 mL
Drops of hot pepper sauce	3	3

(continued on next page)

Put first 4 ingredients into medium bowl. Mix well. Shape into flattened rectangular loaf. Place on ungreased sheet of heavy-duty (or double layer of regular) foil. Fold edges of foil to enclose. Preheat barbecue to medium. Place meatloaf in foil on 1 side of ungreased grill. Turn off burner under meatloaf, leaving opposite burner on medium. Close lid. Cook for about 1 1/4 hours until meatloaf is no longer pink inside.

Combine remaining 5 ingredients in separate medium bowl. Remove meatloaf from grill. Open foil. Spread chili sauce mixture over meatloaf. Return to grill, leaving foil open. Close lid. Cook for about 15 minutes until sauce is bubbling. Serves 6.

1 serving: 338 Calories; 17.4 g Total Fat (7.6 g Mono, 0.8 g Poly, 6.9 g Sat); 64 mg Cholesterol; 23 g Carbohydrate; 3 g Fibre; 23 g Protein; 1317 mg Sodium

Pictured below.

Top: Barbecued Meatloaf, page 68
Bottom: Mustard Seasoned Steak, page 68

The tropical taste comes alive on the barbecue!

serving suggestion

Delicious served with Mushroom Packets, page 110, or Roasted Vegetable Mix, page 112. For garnish, add a few grilled lemon wedges.

Mango-Stuffed Chicken

Diced ripe mango (or 14 oz., 398 mL, can of sliced mango with syrup, drained and diced)	1 cup	250 mL
Finely chopped salted macadamia nuts (or almonds)	1/2 cup	125 mL
Thinly sliced green onion	2 tbsp.	30 mL
Grated lime (or lemon) zest	1/2 tsp.	2 mL
Curry powder	1/2 tsp.	2 mL
Whole roasting chicken	4 lbs.	1.8 kg
LIME YOGURT MARINADE		
Plain yogurt	1 1/2 cups	375 mL
Lime (or lemon) juice	1/4 cup	60 mL
Ground coriander	1 tbsp.	15 mL
Curry powder	1 tbsp.	15 mL
Finely grated, peeled gingerroot (or 1/2 tsp., 2 mL, ground ginger)	2 tsp.	10 mL
Garlic cloves, minced (or 1 tsp., 5 mL, powder)	4	4
Salt	1 tsp.	5 mL

Put first 5 ingredients into medium bowl. Stir.

Place chicken, backbone-up, on cutting board. Cut down both sides of backbone with kitchen shears or sharp knife to remove. Turn chicken over. Press chicken out flat. Carefully loosen skin but do not remove. Stuff mango mixture between meat and skin, spreading mixture as evenly as possible. Place stuffed chicken in large shallow baking dish.

Lime Yogurt Marinade: Combine all 7 ingredients in small bowl. Makes about 1 3/4 cups (425 mL) marinade. Pour over chicken. Turn until coated. Cover with plastic wrap. Marinate in refrigerator for at least 3 hours, turning occasionally. Drain and discard marinade. Preheat barbecue to medium. Place chicken, skin-side down, on 1 side of greased grill over drip pan. Turn off burner under chicken, leaving opposite burner on medium. Close lid. Cook for 45 minutes. Turn chicken over. Close lid. Cook for 45 to 50 minutes until meat thermometer inserted into breast (not stuffing) reads 180°F (82°C). Remove from heat. Cover with foil. Let stand for 15 minutes. Cut into serving-size portions. Serves 6.

1 serving: 399 Calories; 24.1 g Total Fat (12.2 g Mono, 3.7 g Poly, 5.9 g Sat); 107 mg Cholesterol; 10 g Carbohydrate; 2 g Fibre; 35 g Protein; 320 mg Sodium

Pictured on page 71.

The sauce takes on a pretty pink colour from the grenadine. Don't forget to eat the lettuce—it's delightfully refreshing with lemon sauce on it!

Lemon Chicken And Sauce

LEMON MARINADE

Frozen concentrated lemonade, thawed	1/4 cup	60 mL
Cooking oil	1 tbsp.	15 mL
Grenadine syrup	1 tbsp.	15 mL
Onion powder	1/2 tsp.	2 mL
Garlic salt	1/2 tsp.	2 mL
Boneless, skinless chicken breast halves (4 – 6 oz., 113 – 170 g, each)	4	4
Water	1/2 cup	125 mL
Frozen concentrated lemonade, thawed	1/4 cup	60 mL
Grenadine syrup	2 tbsp.	30 mL
Cornstarch	1 tbsp.	15 mL
Grated lemon zest	1 tsp.	5 mL
Chopped iceberg lettuce, lightly packed	2 cups	500 mL

Lemon slices, halved, for garnish

Lemon Marinade: Combine first 5 ingredients in small bowl. Makes about 1/3 cup (75 mL) marinade.

Place chicken in large resealable freezer bag. Add marinade. Seal bag. Turn until coated. Marinate in refrigerator for at least 6 hours or overnight, turning occasionally. Drain and discard marinade. Preheat barbecue to medium. Place chicken on greased grill. Close lid. Cook for 20 to 25 minutes, turning occasionally, until no longer pink inside.

Combine next 5 ingredients in small saucepan. Heat and stir on medium for about 6 minutes until boiling and thickened. Makes about 2/3 cup (150 mL) sauce.

Arrange lettuce on 4 individual plates. Place 1 chicken breast half on top of lettuce on each plate. Spoon sauce over each chicken breast half.

Garnish each serving with lemon slices. Serves 4.

1 serving: 276 Calories; 4.2 g Total Fat (1.6 g Mono, 1.1 g Poly, 0.8 g Sat); 81 mg Cholesterol; 27 g Carbohydrate; trace Fibre; 32 g Protein; 90 mg Sodium

Pictured on page 73.

Skewers with turkey, pineapple and green pepper. Sweet and delicious.

serving suggestion

Serve with rice and fresh green salad on the side.

Teriyaki Turkey Skewers

HONEY TERIYAKI SAUCE

Teriyaki sauce	1/2 cup	125 mL
Liquid honey	2 tbsp.	30 mL
Ketchup	2 tbsp.	30 mL
Pepper	1 tsp.	5 mL
Garlic powder	1/2 tsp.	2 mL
Ground ginger	1/4 – 1/2 tsp.	1 – 2 mL
Cayenne pepper	1/8 – 1/4 tsp.	0.5 – 1 mL
Boneless, skinless turkey breast half, cut into 1 inch (2.5 cm) cubes	1 1/2 lbs.	680 g
Fresh pineapple, cut into 3/4 inch (2 cm) pieces	2 1/2 cups	625 mL
Green medium pepper, seeds and ribs removed, cut into 3/4 inch (2 cm) pieces	2 1/2 cups	625 mL
Bamboo skewers (12 inch, 30 cm, length), soaked in water for 10 minutes	12	12

Honey Teriyaki Sauce: Combine first 7 ingredients in small bowl. Makes about 3/4 cup (175 mL) sauce.

Thread turkey, pineapple and green pepper alternately onto skewers. Preheat barbecue to medium. Cook skewers on greased grill for 12 to 15 minutes, turning occasionally and brushing with sauce, until turkey is no longer pink inside. Makes 12 skewers.

1 skewer: 114 Calories; 0.5 g Total Fat (0.1 g Mono, 0.2 g Poly, 0.1 g Sat); 35 mg Cholesterol; 12 g Carbohydrate; 1 g Fibre; 15 g Protein; 545 mg Sodium

Pictured on front cover and page 75.

The olive oil and fresh herb filling in this roll keeps the turkey moist and succulent.

serving suggestion

Try this with Foiled Yams, page 109, or Roasted Vegetable Mix, page 112.

Herbed Turkey Roll

Boneless, skinless turkey breast half (about 1 1/2 lbs., 680 g)	1	1
Olive (or cooking) oil	3 tbsp.	50 mL
Garlic cloves, minced (or 1 tsp., 5 mL, powder)	4	4
Dijon mustard	1 tbsp.	15 mL
Chopped fresh parsley (or 3/4 tsp., 4 mL, flakes)	1 tbsp.	15 mL
Chopped fresh chives (or 3/4 tsp., 4 mL, dried)	1 tbsp.	15 mL
Fresh rosemary leaves (or 1/4 – 3/4 tsp., 2 – 4 mL, dried, crushed)	1 – 3 tsp.	5 – 15 mL
Salt	1 tsp.	5 mL
Pepper	1 tsp.	5 mL
Uncooked bacon slices	3 – 4	3 – 4

Butterfly turkey breast half by cutting horizontally through middle, not quite to other side. Spread open and pound with smooth side of mallet until thin, even thickness.

Combine next 8 ingredients in small bowl. Spread evenly on turkey breast half. Roll up tightly, starting from long edge. Secure with butcher's string.

Lay bacon slices over top of turkey roll. Preheat barbecue to medium. Place turkey roll on 1 side of greased grill over drip pan. Turn off burner under drip pan, leaving opposite burner on medium. Close lid. Cook for about 1 1/2 hours until turkey is no longer pink inside. Remove to platter. Remove and discard string. Discard bacon if desired. Slice turkey roll into 3/4 inch (2 cm) thick slices. Serves 4.

1 serving: 317 Calories; 14 g Total Fat (8.9 g Mono, 1.6 g Poly, 2.6 g Sat); 109 mg Cholesterol; 2 g Carbohydrate; trace Fibre; 44 g Protein; 806 mg Sodium

Pictured on page 77.

These tender, browned Cornish hens taste of apple and sage with a hint of cinnamon. A great meal for entertaining.

serving suggestion

Serve with wild rice and your favourite vegetable.

Roasted Cornish Hens

Cornish hens (about 1 1/2 lbs., 680 g, each)	2	2
BEER MARINADE		
Beer (or alcohol-free beer)	1 cup	250 mL
Applesauce	1/2 cup	125 mL
Olive (or cooking) oil	2 tbsp.	30 mL
Liquid honey	2 tbsp.	30 mL
Paprika	1 tsp.	5 mL
Ground sage	3/4 tsp.	4 mL
Ground cinnamon	1/2 tsp.	2 mL
Salt	1/4 tsp.	1 mL

Place 1 Cornish hen, backbone-up, on cutting board. Cut down both sides of backbone with kitchen shears or sharp knife to remove. Turn hen over. Cut lengthwise through breast into halves. Repeat with remaining hen.

Beer Marinade: Combine all 8 ingredients in large bowl. Makes about 1 3/4 cups (425 mL) marinade. Add Cornish hen halves. Turn until coated. Cover with plastic wrap. Marinate in refrigerator for at least 6 hours or overnight, turning occasionally. Drain, reserving marinade in small saucepan. Bring reserved marinade to a boil on medium. Reduce heat to medium-low. Simmer, uncovered, for at least 5 minutes. Preheat barbecue to high. Place Cornish hen halves, bone-side down, on 1 side of greased grill. Turn off burner under hen halves, leaving opposite burner on medium. Brush hen halves with reserved marinade. Close lid. Cook for 20 minutes. Turn. Close lid. Cook for about 20 minutes, turning occasionally and brushing with marinade, until browned and no longer pink inside. Serves 4.

1 serving: 435 Calories; 27.8 g Total Fat (14.2 g Mono, 4.8 g Poly, 6.7 g Sat); 150 mg Cholesterol; 15 g Carbohydrate; 1 g Fibre; 26 g Protein; 226 mg Sodium

Pictured on page 79.

You will love the light smoky flavour of this salmon, perfectly complemented by delicately sweet maple syrup.

Cedar Plank Salmon

Cedar planks (see Note)	2	2
Water		
WHISKY MARINADE		
Canadian whisky (rye)	1 cup	250 mL
Maple (or maple-flavoured) syrup	1/2 cup	125 mL
Soy sauce	1/3 cup	75 mL
Olive (or cooking) oil	1/4 cup	60 mL
Parsley flakes	1/4 cup	60 mL
Sweet (or regular) chili sauce	3 tbsp.	50 mL
Pepper	1 tsp.	5 mL
Salmon fillets (about 4 oz., 113 g, each), or side of salmon (about 2 lbs., 900 g), skin removed, cut into 8 equal pieces	8	8

Place cedar planks in large container. Add enough water to cover. Weight planks with heavy cans to keep submerged. Let stand for at least 6 hours or overnight to soak.

Whisky Marinade: Combine first 7 ingredients in medium bowl. Makes about 2 1/4 cups (550 mL) marinade.

Place salmon in large shallow baking dish. Pour marinade over top. Turn until coated. Cover. Marinate in refrigerator for at least 30 minutes, turning occasionally. Drain and discard marinade. Preheat barbecue to medium-low. Place salmon on cedar planks on ungreased grill. Close lid. Cook for 15 to 30 minutes until salmon flakes easily when tested with fork. Serves 8.

1 serving: 260 Calories; 10.6 g Total Fat (4.9 g Mono, 3.2 g Poly, 1.6 g Sat); 62 mg Cholesterol; 9 g Carbohydrate; trace Fibre; 23 g Protein; 457 mg Sodium

Pictured on page 81.

This is a wonderful way to prepare a piece of whole salmon. Smothered in a buttery lemon barbecue sauce.

Salmon Supreme

LEMON BARBECUE SAUCE

Lemon juice	2/3 cup	150 mL
Hickory barbecue sauce	1/2 cup	125 mL
Butter (or hard margarine)	1/2 cup	125 mL
Finely chopped onion	1/4 cup	60 mL
Brown sugar, packed	1/2 tbsp.	7 mL
Garlic powder, just a pinch		
Centre section of whole salmon (with skin), cut lengthwise to backbone and opened flat	3 lbs.	1.4 kg

Lemon Barbecue Sauce: Combine first 6 ingredients in small saucepan. Bring to a boil on medium. Reduce heat to medium-low. Simmer, uncovered, for 20 to 30 minutes, stirring often, until onion is softened. Makes about 1 cup (250 mL) sauce.

Brush salmon flesh with 1/2 of sauce. Preheat barbecue to medium. Place salmon, flesh-side down, on greased grill. Close lid. Cook for 15 minutes. Turn. Brush salmon flesh with remaining 1/2 of sauce. Close lid. Cook for about 12 minutes, without turning, until salmon flakes easily when tested with fork. Cut into 10 equal portions. Serves 10.

1 serving: 275 Calories; 17.6 g Total Fat (5.4 g Mono, 3.5 g Poly, 7.3 g Sat); 92 mg Cholesterol; 4 g Carbohydrate; 1 g Fibre; 24 g Protein; 260 mg Sodium

Pictured on page 83.

*Try salmon this way for a change.
A treat to remember!*

Teriyaki Salmon

TERIYAKI MARINADE

Soy sauce	3/4 cup	175 mL
Brown sugar, packed	1/2 cup	125 mL
Cooking oil	2 tbsp.	30 mL
Ground ginger	1/2 tsp.	2 mL
Garlic powder	1/4 tsp.	1 mL
Salmon steaks (or fillets), about 5 oz. (140 g) each	4	4

Teriyaki Marinade: Combine first 5 ingredients in small bowl. Makes about 1 cup (250 mL) marinade.

Place salmon steaks in large shallow baking dish. Pour marinade over top. Turn until coated. Cover. Marinate in refrigerator for 30 minutes, turning occasionally. Drain and discard marinade. Preheat barbecue to medium. Cook salmon steaks on greased grill for about 5 minutes per side until salmon flakes easily when tested with fork. Serves 4.

1 serving: 303 Calories; 12.3 g Total Fat (5 g Mono, 4.6 g Poly, 1.6 g Sat); 77 mg Cholesterol; 17 g Carbohydrate; trace Fibre; 30 g Protein; 1703 mg Sodium

Pictured on page 85.

Zesty lemon marinade perfectly accents this moist fish. Delicate sea bass should be turned carefully to avoid breaking.

Lemon Dill Bass

LEMON DILL MARINADE

Lemon juice	1/4 cup	60 mL
Olive (or cooking) oil	2 tbsp.	30 mL
Chopped fresh dill (or 1 1/4 tsp., 6 mL, dill weed)	1 1/2 tbsp.	25 mL
Chopped fresh chives (or 3/4 tsp., 4 mL, dried)	1 tbsp.	15 mL
Grated lemon zest	2 tsp.	10 mL
Paprika	1 tsp.	5 mL
Salt	1/2 tsp.	2 mL
Fresh (or frozen, thawed) sea bass steaks	1 1/4 lbs.	560 g

(continued on next page)

Lemon Dill Marinade: Combine first 7 ingredients in small bowl. Makes about 1/3 cup (75 mL) marinade.

Place bass steaks in shallow medium baking dish. Pour marinade over top. Turn until coated. Cover. Marinate in refrigerator for 30 minutes, turning occasionally. Drain and discard marinade. Preheat barbecue to medium. Cook bass steaks on greased grill for 15 to 20 minutes, turning once, until bass flakes easily when tested with fork. Cut bass steaks into 4 equal portions, removing and discarding skin and bones. Serves 4.

1 serving: 170 Calories; 6.3 g Total Fat (3.1 g Mono, 1.4 g Poly, 1.2 g Sat); 57 mg Cholesterol; 1 g Carbohydrate; trace Fibre; 26 g Protein; 244 mg Sodium

Pictured below.

Left: Teriyaki Salmon, page 84
Right: Lemon Dill Bass, page 84

Slightly sweet apricot and dill filling is a delectable complement to trout.

note

To toast nuts, spread evenly in ungreased shallow pan. Bake in 350°F (175°C) oven for 5 to 10 minutes, stirring or shaking often, until desired doneness.

Apricot-Stuffed Trout

Cooking oil	2 tsp.	10 mL
Finely chopped red onion	1/4 cup	60 mL
Cooked jasmine (or long grain white) rice	1/2 cup	125 mL
Finely chopped pecans, toasted (see Note)	2 tbsp.	30 mL
Orange juice	1 tbsp.	15 mL
Finely chopped dried apricot	1 tbsp.	15 mL
Chopped fresh dill (or 1/2 tsp., 2 mL, dill weed)	1 1/2 tsp.	7 mL
Salt	1/4 tsp.	1 mL
Pepper, just a pinch		
Whole trout (about 10 oz., 280 g, each), pan ready	2	2

Heat cooking oil in small frying pan on medium. Add onion. Cook for 5 to 10 minutes, stirring often, until softened. Transfer to large bowl.

Add next 7 ingredients. Stir well.

Rinse inside of each trout. Pat dry with paper towels. Divide and spoon rice mixture into each trout. Spread evenly. Tie each with butcher's string or secure with metal skewers to enclose filling. Preheat barbecue to medium-low. Place trout on greased grill. Close lid. Cook for 5 to 6 minutes per side until trout flakes easily when tested with fork. Serves 4.

1 serving: *236 Calories; 11.4 g Total Fat (6.1 g Mono, 2.8 g Poly, 1.5 g Sat); 57 mg Cholesterol; 11 g Carbohydrate; trace Fibre; 22 g Protein; 200 mg Sodium*

Pictured on page 87.

These tender, grilled scallops, delicately coated with lightly spiced honey mustard sauce, are sure to impress!

Sweet Scallop Skewers

Fresh (or frozen, thawed) large sea scallops, cut into 1/2 inch (12 mm) thick pieces	1 lb.	454 g
Bamboo skewers (8 inch, 20 cm, length), soaked in water for 10 minutes	8	8
Liquid honey	2 tbsp.	30 mL
Dijon mustard	2 tbsp.	30 mL
Grated orange zest	1/4 tsp.	1 mL
Chili powder	1/4 tsp.	1 mL
Salt	1/4 tsp.	1 mL

Thread scallop pieces onto skewers.

Combine remaining 5 ingredients in small bowl. Brush scallop pieces with honey mixture. Preheat barbecue to medium. Cook skewers on greased grill for about 8 minutes, turning occasionally and brushing with remaining honey mixture, until scallop pieces are opaque. Do not overcook. Makes 8 skewers.

1 skewer: 70 Calories; 0.7 g Total Fat (0.1 g Mono, 0.3 g Poly, 0.1 g Sat); 19 mg Cholesterol; 6 g Carbohydrate; trace Fibre; 10 g Protein; 219 mg Sodium

Pictured on page 89.

Colourful cantaloupe salsa is a delightful condiment for tuna. Avoid overcooking tuna to prevent drying.

Tuna Skewers

CANTALOUPE SALSA

Diced cantaloupe	1 cup	250 mL
Finely chopped green onion	2 tbsp.	30 mL
Lemon juice	1 1/2 tbsp.	25 mL
Cooking oil	1 tbsp.	15 mL
Chopped fresh basil	1 tbsp.	15 mL
Salt	1/4 tsp.	1 mL
Pepper, just a pinch		
Lemon juice	1/4 cup	60 mL
Soy sauce	2 tbsp.	30 mL
Brown sugar, packed	2 tbsp.	30 mL
Garlic clove, minced (or 1/4 tsp., 1 mL, powder)	1	1

(continued on next page)

Tuna steaks (or fillets), cut into 1 inch (2.5 cm) cubes	1 3/4 lbs.	790 g
Bamboo skewers (8 inch, 20 cm, length), soaked in water for 10 minutes	8	8

Cantaloupe Salsa: Combine first 7 ingredients in medium bowl. Cover. Chill for 2 hours to blend flavours. Drain and discard liquid. Transfer solids to small serving dish. Makes about 1 cup (250 mL) salsa.

Combine next 4 ingredients in small bowl.

Thread tuna cubes onto skewers. Brush with lemon juice mixture. Preheat barbecue to medium. Cook skewers on greased grill for about 5 minutes, turning occasionally and brushing with remaining lemon juice mixture, until tuna is firm and no longer opaque. Serve with Cantaloupe Salsa. Serves 8.

1 serving: 141 Calories; 1.9 g Total Fat (0.7 g Mono, 0.5 g Poly, 0.3 g Sat); 44 mg Cholesterol; 7 g Carbohydrate; trace Fibre; 24 g Protein; 340 mg Sodium

Pictured below.

Left: Tuna Skewers, page 88
Top Centre: Cantaloupe Salsa, page 89
Right: Sweet Scallop Skewers, page 88

Sweet, tangy marinade makes pork tenderloin especially tasty!

note

When grilling, always use tongs to turn meat. Using a fork will pierce the meat and natural juices will run out, causing meat to be drier.

Barbecued Tenderloin Slices

CHILI MARINADE

Sweet (or regular) chili sauce	1/2 cup	125 mL
Ketchup	1/2 cup	125 mL
Apple cider vinegar	1/2 cup	125 mL
Fancy (mild) molasses	1/3 cup	75 mL
Lemon juice	1 tbsp.	15 mL
Worcestershire sauce	2 tsp.	10 mL
Dry mustard	2 tsp.	10 mL
Pork tenderloins (about 1 lb., 454 g, each), trimmed of fat	2	2

Chili Marinade: Combine first 7 ingredients in small bowl. Makes about 2 cups (500 mL) marinade.

Cut each tenderloin almost in half lengthwise, but not quite through to other side. Press open to flatten. Place in large resealable freezer bag. Pour 1/2 of marinade over tenderloins. Chill remaining marinade. Seal bag. Turn until coated. Marinate in refrigerator for at least 4 hours, turning occasionally. Drain and discard marinade. Preheat barbecue to medium. Place tenderloins on greased grill. Close lid. Cook for about 20 minutes, turning occasionally (see Note) and brushing with remaining marinade, until meat thermometer inserted into thickest part of tenderloin reads 155°F (68°C). Remove from heat. Cover with foil. Let stand for 10 minutes. Internal temperature should rise to at least 160°F (70°C). Cut each tenderloin into 1/2 inch (12 mm) thick slices. Serves 8.

1 serving: 199 Calories; 5 g Total Fat (2.2 g Mono, 0.4 g Poly, 1.6 g Sat); 66 mg Cholesterol; 15 g Carbohydrate; 1 g Fibre; 23 g Protein; 378 mg Sodium

Pictured on page 91.

The peppery marinade is a real winner! Marinate pork overnight to infuse with even more flavour.

serving suggestion

Serve with Veggie Pasta Salad, page 44, or Mushroom Packets, page 110.

Best Pork Chops

GARLIC MARINADE

Water	1/2 cup	125 mL
Soy sauce	1/3 cup	75 mL
Cooking oil	1/4 cup	60 mL
Lemon pepper	3 tbsp.	50 mL
Garlic cloves, minced (or 1/2 tsp., 2 mL, powder)	2	2
Bone-in pork chops (about 2 1/2 lbs., 1.1 kg), trimmed of fat	6	6

Garlic Marinade: Combine first 5 ingredients in small bowl. Makes about 1 cup (250 mL) marinade.

Place pork chops in single layer in large shallow baking dish. Pour marinade over top. Turn until coated. Cover. Marinate in refrigerator for 45 minutes, turning occasionally. Drain, reserving marinade in small saucepan. Bring reserved marinade to a boil on medium. Reduce heat to medium-low. Simmer, uncovered, for at least 5 minutes. Preheat barbecue to medium. Cook pork chops on greased grill for about 25 minutes, turning once and brushing with reserved marinade, until desired doneness. Serves 6.

1 serving: 274 Calories; 15.9 g Total Fat (8.5 g Mono, 3.5 g Poly, 2.8 g Sat); 77 mg Cholesterol; 3 g Carbohydrate; trace Fibre; 29 g Protein; 2824 mg Sodium

Pictured on page 95.

Minted Lamb Chops

RED WINE MARINADE

Dry red (or alcohol-free) wine	1/2 cup	125 mL
Mint jelly	1/3 cup	75 mL
Lemon juice	3 tbsp.	50 mL
Finely grated, peeled gingerroot (or 1/8 tsp., 0.5 mL, ground ginger)	1/2 tsp.	2 mL
Salt	1/2 tsp.	2 mL
Pepper	1/2 tsp.	2 mL
Lamb loin chops (2 – 2 1/2 lbs., 900 g – 1.1 kg)	12	12

Red wine and a hint of mint make a delectable marinade for tender lamb. Use your favourite cut of lamb chops and adjust cooking time to suit.

Red Wine Marinade: Heat and stir first 6 ingredients in medium saucepan on medium for about 5 minutes until smooth. Cool. Makes about 1 cup (250 mL) marinade.

Arrange lamb chops in single layer in large shallow baking dish. Pour marinade over top. Turn until coated. Cover. Marinate in refrigerator for 6 hours or overnight, turning occasionally. Drain and discard marinade. Preheat barbecue to medium. Cook lamb chops on greased grill for 5 to 7 minutes per side until desired doneness. Serves 6.

1 serving: 436 Calories; 29.6 g Total Fat (12.4 g Mono, 2.2 g Poly, 12.6 g Sat); 128 mg Cholesterol; 7 g Carbohydrate; trace Fibre; 32 g Protein; 202 mg Sodium

Pictured on pages 94/95.

Photo Legend, next page

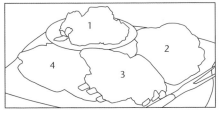

1. Minted Lamb Chops, above
2. Best Pork Chops, page 92
3. Java Ribs, page 97
4. Honey Ham Steaks, page 96

A foolproof meal that is quick and easy to prepare.

serving suggestion

Serve with Quick Corn, page 102, or Veggie Bread Kabobs, page 104.

Honey Ham Steaks

HONEY MUSTARD SAUCE

Brown sugar, packed	1/4 cup	60 mL
Hard margarine (or butter)	1/4 cup	60 mL
Liquid honey	1 tbsp.	15 mL
Soy sauce	1 tsp.	5 mL
Prepared mustard	1 tsp.	5 mL
Ham steaks, trimmed of fat (about 2 lbs., 900 g)	8	8

Honey Mustard Sauce: Heat and stir first 5 ingredients in small saucepan on medium for about 5 minutes until sugar is dissolved. Makes about 3/4 cup (175 mL) sauce. Transfer 1/2 cup (125 mL) sauce to small serving dish. Set aside to serve with ham.

Preheat barbecue to medium-high. Place ham steaks on greased grill. Brush steaks with about 2 tbsp. (30 mL) remaining sauce. Cook for about 5 minutes until lightly browned. Turn. Brush with remaining sauce. Cook for 2 to 3 minutes until glazed and heated through. Serves 8.

1 serving: 228 Calories; 10.9 g Total Fat (6.2 g Mono, 1.2 g Poly, 2.9 g Sat); 51 mg Cholesterol; 9 g Carbohydrate; 0 g Fibre; 22 g Protein; 1555 mg Sodium

Pictured on page 94.

Java Ribs

Pork spareribs, cut into 3-bone portions	6 lbs.	2.7 kg
Water		
Bay leaves	2	2
Dried thyme	3/4 tsp.	4 mL
Onion salt	1/2 tsp.	2 mL
Pepper	1/2 tsp.	2 mL
COFFEE MARINADE		
Cold strong prepared coffee	1 1/4 cups	300 mL
Ketchup	1 1/4 cups	300 mL
Brown sugar, packed	2/3 cup	150 mL
Apple cider vinegar	1/2 cup	125 mL
Worcestershire sauce	4 tsp.	20 mL

The unique marinade, made with coffee, transforms tender pork ribs into a succulent feast!

Place ribs in large pot or Dutch oven. Add enough water to cover. Add next 4 ingredients. Bring to a boil on medium-high. Reduce heat to medium-low. Cover. Simmer for about 1 hour until pork is just tender. Drain and discard liquid. Cool.

Coffee Marinade: Measure all 5 ingredients into large bowl. Stir until sugar is dissolved. Makes about 3 1/2 cups (875 mL) marinade. Add ribs. Turn until coated. Cover. Let stand for 30 minutes. Drain, reserving marinade in medium saucepan. Bring reserved marinade to a boil on medium. Reduce heat to medium-low. Simmer, uncovered, for at least 5 minutes. Preheat barbecue to medium. Cook ribs on greased grill for 15 to 20 minutes, turning occasionally and brushing with reserved marinade, until glazed and heated through. Serves 8.

1 serving: 500 Calories; 26.5 g Total Fat (11.8 g Mono, 2.4 g Poly, 9.7 g Sat); 128 mg Cholesterol; 31 g Carbohydrate; 1 g Fibre; 34 g Protein; 622 mg Sodium

Pictured on pages 94/95.

Fragrant and tender—these will have everyone asking for more!

note

To bruise cardamom, hit cardamom pods with mallet or flat side of wide knife to "bruise" or crack them open slightly.

Lamb Kabobs

LEMON GINGER MARINADE

Cooking oil	1/2 cup	125 mL
Lemon juice	1/4 cup	60 mL
Ground ginger	3/4 tsp.	4 mL
Garlic powder	1/2 tsp.	2 mL
Paprika	1/2 tsp.	2 mL
Whole green cardamom, bruised (see Note)	5	5
Pepper	1/8 tsp.	0.5 mL
Lamb stew meat	1 1/2 lbs.	680 g
Medium onion, cut into 1 inch (2.5 cm) pieces	1	1
Green medium pepper, seeds and ribs removed, cut into 1 inch (2.5 cm) pieces	1	1
Bamboo skewers (8 inch, 20 cm, length), soaked in water for 10 minutes	12	12

Salt, sprinkle

Lemon Ginger Marinade: Combine first 7 ingredients in large bowl. Makes about 3/4 cup (175 mL) marinade.

Add lamb, onion and green pepper. Stir until coated. Cover. Marinate in refrigerator for 3 1/2 to 4 hours, stirring occasionally. Drain, reserving marinade in small saucepan. Bring reserved marinade to a boil on medium. Reduce heat to medium-low. Simmer, uncovered, for at least 5 minutes.

Thread lamb, onion and green pepper alternately onto skewers. Preheat barbecue to medium-high. Cook kabobs on greased grill for 15 to 20 minutes, turning occasionally and brushing with reserved marinade, until desired doneness.

Sprinkle with salt. Makes 12 kabobs.

1 kabob: 171 Calories; 12.7 g Total Fat (6.9 g Mono, 3.1 g Poly, 1.8 g Sat); 37 mg Cholesterol; 2 g Carbohydrate; trace Fibre; 12 g Protein; 32 mg Sodium

Pictured on page 99.

Wieners and sauerkraut are a natural pair.

Frankly Sauerkraut

Wieners	12	12
Prepared mustard	2 tbsp.	30 mL
Sauerkraut, drained	1 1/2 cups	375 mL
Ketchup (optional)	2 tbsp.	30 mL
Hot dog buns, split and toasted (buttered, optional)	12	12
Chopped onion, cooked if desired	1 cup	250 mL

Slice each wiener almost in half lengthwise, but not quite through to other side. Press open. Spread 1/2 tsp. (2 mL) mustard evenly on both cut sides of each wiener. Place 1 wiener, cut-side up, on each of 12 individual sheets of heavy-duty (or double layer of regular) foil. Spoon about 2 tbsp. (30 mL) sauerkraut onto each wiener. Spread evenly. Fold edges of foil to enclose. Preheat barbecue to medium. Place packets on ungreased grill. Close lid. Cook for about 5 minutes, turning once, until heated through. Remove and discard foil.

Spread 1/2 tsp. (2 mL) ketchup evenly on top half of each bun. Place 1 wiener on bottom half of each bun. Top each with onion. Cover each with top half of bun. Makes 12 hot dogs.

1 hot dog: 245 Calories; 11.2 g Total Fat (5.3 g Mono, 1.3 g Poly, 3.8 g Sat); 19 mg Cholesterol; 27 g Carbohydrate; trace Fibre; 8 g Protein; 855 mg Sodium

Pictured on page 101.

Use fine wire to secure husks to corncobs, if necessary, to keep in place for grilling.

corn in foil

Remove and discard husks and silk from corncobs. Place 1 cob on each of 6 individual sheets of heavy-duty (or double layer of regular) foil. Spread margarine on cobs. Sprinkle each with salt and pepper. Fold edges of foil to enclose. Place on ungreased grill. Close lid. Cook for about 12 minutes, turning cobs 1/4 turn every 3 minutes, until tender.

husky corn

Cook corncobs with husks and silk intact on ungreased grill for about 12 minutes, turning 1/4 turn every 3 minutes, until tender. Remove and discard husks and silk. Spread margarine on cobs. Sprinkle each with salt and pepper.

Quick Corn

Medium corncobs in husks	6	6
Hard margarine (or butter), softened	1/2 cup	125 mL
Salt, sprinkle		
Pepper, sprinkle		

Pull husks down to end of corncobs, leaving them attached to cobs. Remove and discard silk. Spread margarine evenly on cobs. Sprinkle each with salt and pepper. Bring husks back up to cover cobs. Preheat barbecue to medium. Place cobs on ungreased grill. Close lid. Cook for about 12 minutes, turning cobs 1/4 turn every 3 minutes, until tender. Remove and discard husks. Serves 6.

1 serving: 274 Calories; 17.6 g Total Fat (10.9 g Mono, 2.3 g Poly, 3.5 g Sat); 0 mg Cholesterol; 31 g Carbohydrate; 4 g Fibre; 4 g Protein; 209 mg Sodium

Pictured on page 103.

Tender, colourful vegetables and toasted bread cubes make a wonderful kabob combination.

Veggie Bread Kabobs

BALSAMIC SAUCE

Olive (or cooking) oil	1/3 cup	75 mL
Balsamic vinegar	3 tbsp.	50 mL
Sun-dried tomatoes in oil, drained	2 tbsp.	30 mL
Coarsely chopped fresh parsley (or 1 1/2 tsp., 7 mL, flakes)	2 tbsp.	30 mL
Liquid honey	1 tbsp.	15 mL
Garlic clove (or 1/4 tsp., 1 mL, powder)	1	1
Salt	1/4 tsp.	1 mL
Medium zucchini (with peel), cut into 1/2 inch (12 mm) thick slices	2	2
Fresh whole white mushrooms	20	20
Red medium peppers, seeds and ribs removed, cut into 1 inch (2.5 cm) pieces	2	2
Sourdough bread loaf, cut into 1 inch (2.5 cm) cubes	1	1
Bamboo skewers (10 inch, 25 cm, length), soaked in water for 10 minutes	10	10

Balsamic Sauce: Process first 7 ingredients in blender or food processor until smooth. Makes about 3/4 cup (175 mL) sauce.

Thread zucchini, mushrooms, red pepper and bread cubes alternately onto skewers. Place in single layer in large shallow baking dish. Brush kabobs with sauce. Cover. Let stand for 30 minutes. Preheat barbecue to medium. Cook kabobs on greased grill for about 15 minutes, turning occasionally, until bread is crisp and vegetables are tender. Makes 10 kabobs.

1 kabob: 225 Calories; 9.4 g Total Fat (6.3 g Mono, 1.1 g Poly, 1.4 g Sat); 0 mg Cholesterol; 31 g Carbohydrate; 3 g Fibre; 6 g Protein; 343 mg Sodium

Pictured on page 106.

Vegetable Skewers With Pesto Dressing

PESTO DRESSING

Fresh basil leaves	3/4 cup	175 mL
Italian salad dressing	1/4 cup	60 mL
Grated Parmesan cheese	3 tbsp.	50 mL
Pine nuts, toasted (see Note)	2 tbsp.	30 mL
Garlic clove, chopped (or 1/4 tsp., 1 mL, powder)	1	1
Salt	1/8 tsp.	0.5 mL
Pepper	1/4 tsp.	1 mL
Medium zucchini (with peel), cut into 3/4 inch (2 cm) cubes	1 – 2	1 – 2
Red medium pepper, seeds and ribs removed, cut into 1 inch (2.5 cm) pieces	1	1
Yellow medium pepper, seeds and ribs removed, cut into 1 inch (2.5 cm) pieces	1	1
Small red onion, cut into wedges	1	1
Metal skewers (10 inch, 25 cm, length), or bamboo skewers (10 inch, 25 cm, length), soaked in water for 10 minutes	6	6

Pesto Dressing: Process first 7 ingredients in blender or food processor until smooth. Makes about 1/2 cup (125 mL) dressing.

Put next 4 ingredients into large bowl. Toss gently. Add 1/4 cup (60 mL) dressing to vegetable mixture. Toss gently. Set remaining dressing aside.

Thread vegetables alternately onto skewers. Preheat barbecue to medium. Cook skewers on greased grill for 12 to 15 minutes, turning occasionally, until vegetables are tender-crisp. Serve with remaining dressing. Makes 6 skewers.

1 skewer with 2 tsp. (10 mL) dressing: 122 Calories; 10.1 g Total Fat (4.9 g Mono, 3.2 g Poly, 1.4 g Sat); 9 mg Cholesterol; 7 g Carbohydrate; 2 g Fibre; 3 g Protein; 278 mg Sodium

Pictured on divider.

Colourful vegetables glistening on the barbecue are bound to attract the attention of your guests. Make the pesto dressing ahead of time to blend flavours.

note

To toast nuts, spread evenly in ungreased shallow pan. Bake in 350°F (175°C) oven for 5 to 10 minutes, stirring or shaking often, until desired doneness.

Photo Legend, next page
Top Left: Foiled Yams, page 109
Centre Right: Potatoes On A Stick, page 108
Bottom Left: Veggie Bread Kabobs, page 104

It's so easy to make potatoes special for summer barbecues and patio parties. Vary this recipe by using fresh herbs, such as chives or summer savory, in place of dried.

Potatoes On A Stick

Red baby potatoes (with skin), larger ones cut in half	10	10
White baby potatoes (with skin), larger ones cut in half	10	10
Water		
Olive (or cooking) oil	2 tbsp.	30 mL
Seasoned salt	1 tsp.	5 mL
Dried basil	1/2 tsp.	2 mL
Dried whole oregano	1/2 tsp.	2 mL
Dried rosemary, crushed	1/8 tsp.	0.5 mL
Pepper, sprinkle		
Metal skewers (12 inch, 30 cm, length)	4	4

Cook potatoes in water in medium saucepan until tender but still firm. Drain. Let stand until cool enough to handle.

Combine next 6 ingredients in small bowl.

Thread potatoes, alternating red and white, onto skewers, using 5 potatoes for each. Brush potatoes with olive oil mixture. Preheat barbecue to high. Place skewers on greased grill. Close lid. Cook for about 30 minutes, turning occasionally and brushing with remaining olive oil mixture, until desired doneness. Makes 4 skewers.

1 skewer: 200 Calories; 7.1 g Total Fat (5.1 g Mono, 0.7 g Poly, 1 g Sat); 0 mg Cholesterol; 31 g Carbohydrate; 3 g Fibre; 4 g Protein; 310 mg Sodium

Pictured on page 107.

Foiled Yams

Medium yams (or sweet potatoes), peeled	4	4
Hard margarine (or butter), softened	2 tbsp.	30 mL
Salt, sprinkle		
Pepper, sprinkle		

Cut 1 yam crosswise into 1/4 to 1/2 inch (6 to 12 mm) thick slices. Place slices on 1 sheet of heavy-duty (or double layer of regular) foil. Dab 1 1/2 tsp. (7 mL) margarine randomly on yam slices. Sprinkle with salt and pepper. Fold edges of foil to enclose. Repeat with remaining yams, margarine, salt and pepper, for a total of 4 packets. Preheat barbecue to medium. Place packets on ungreased grill. Close lid. Cook for 15 to 20 minutes, turning once, until yam is tender. Serves 4.

1 serving: 205 Calories; 6 g Total Fat (3.8 g Mono, 0.7 g Poly, 1.2 g Sat); 0 mg Cholesterol; 36 g Carbohydrate; 5 g Fibre; 2 g Protein; 80 mg Sodium

Pictured on page 106.

A tasty, easy-to-make side dish to add to your favourite barbecue menu.

grilled yams

Cut yams crosswise into 1/2 to 3/4 inch (12 to 20 mm) thick slices. Brush 1 side of each slice with cooking oil. Preheat barbecue to medium. Place yam slices, brushed-side down, on greased grill. Brush top sides with cooking oil. Close lid. Cook for 8 to 10 minutes per side until yam is tender. Serves 4.

foiled turnips

Cook turnips as for Foiled Yams, increasing cooking time to 20 to 25 minutes.

Creamy sauce smothers mushrooms cooked to perfection in foil packets. A terrific accompaniment for Best Pork Chops, page 92.

Mushroom Packets

Hard margarine (or butter)	2 tbsp.	30 mL
Finely chopped onion	1/2 cup	125 mL
All-purpose flour	1 tbsp.	15 mL
Chicken bouillon powder	1 tsp.	5 mL
Paprika	1/4 tsp.	1 mL
Salt	1/4 tsp.	1 mL
Pepper, sprinkle		
Sour cream	1/2 cup	125 mL
Small fresh whole white mushrooms	1 lb.	454 g

Melt margarine in medium frying pan on medium. Add onion. Cook for 5 to 10 minutes, stirring often, until softened.

Add next 5 ingredients. Heat and stir for 1 minute. Slowly add sour cream, stirring constantly, until boiling and thickened. Cool.

Divide and place mushrooms on each of 4 individual sheets of heavy-duty (or double layer of regular) foil. Divide and spoon sour cream mixture over top of each. Fold edges of foil to enclose. Preheat barbecue to medium. Place packets on ungreased grill. Close lid. Cook for 8 to 10 minutes, rotating once, until heated through. Serves 4.

1 serving: 144 Calories; 10.7 g Total Fat (5.1 g Mono, 1 g Poly, 3.9 g Sat); 12 mg Cholesterol; 10 g Carbohydrate; 2 g Fibre; 4 g Protein; 397 mg Sodium

Pictured on page 111.

These tender-crisp asparagus spears are very appetizing.

Barbecued Asparagus

Vanilla (or plain) yogurt	1/4 cup	60 mL
Lemon pepper	2 tsp.	10 mL
White vinegar	1/2 tsp.	2 mL
Cooking oil	1/2 tsp.	2 mL
Fresh asparagus, trimmed of tough ends	1 lb.	454 g

(continued on next page)

Combine first 4 ingredients in small cup.

Preheat barbecue to medium. Arrange asparagus spears crosswise in single layer on greased grill. Lightly brush asparagus with yogurt mixture. Cook for 2 minutes. Brush asparagus with yogurt mixture, gently turning spears 1/4 turn. Cook for 1 to 2 minutes. Brush and turn twice more, cooking for 1 to 2 minutes after each turn, until asparagus is glazed and tender-crisp. Serves 6.

1 serving: 29 Calories; 0.7 g Total Fat (0.3 g Mono, 0.2 g Poly, 0.2 g Sat); 1 mg Cholesterol; 5 g Carbohydrate; 1 g Fibre; 2 g Protein; 403 mg Sodium

Pictured below.

Top: Mushroom Packets, page 110
Bottom: Barbecued Asparagus, page 110

A hearty mixture of root vegetables. Roasting intensifies the natural flavour of each fresh ingredient.

Roasted Vegetable Mix

Yellow turnip (rutabaga), peeled, cut into 1 inch (2.5 cm) cubes	2 1/2 cups	625 mL
Baby carrots	36	36
Medium potatoes (with skin), quartered	5	5
Medium onions, quartered	3	3
Hard margarine (or butter)	3 tbsp.	50 mL
Olive (or cooking) oil	1 tbsp.	15 mL
Water	1 tbsp.	15 mL
Garlic cloves, minced (or 1/2 tsp., 2 mL, powder)	2	2
Dried whole oregano	1 tsp.	5 mL
Dried thyme	1 tsp.	5 mL
Dried rosemary, crushed	1 tsp.	5 mL
Seasoned salt	1 tsp.	5 mL
Pepper, sprinkle		

Place first 4 ingredients in large greased foil pan. Toss.

Melt margarine in small saucepan on low. Add remaining 8 ingredients. Stir. Drizzle over vegetable mixture. Toss until coated. Cover with foil. Preheat barbecue to high. Place pan on 1 side of ungreased grill. Turn burner under pan to low, turning opposite burner down to medium. Close lid. Cook for about 30 minutes, shaking pan occasionally, until vegetables are heated through. Remove foil. Stir. Close lid. Cook for about 30 minutes until vegetables are tender and starting to brown. Serves 6.

1 serving: 240 Calories; 8.6 g Total Fat (5.5 g Mono, 1 g Poly, 1.6 g Sat); 0 mg Cholesterol; 38 g Carbohydrate; 6 g Fibre; 5 g Protein; 343 mg Sodium

Pictured on page 113.

Fresh, glazed peaches with visible grill marks. Delicious served with grilled croissants and ice cream.

Balsamic Peaches

Fresh peaches (with skin), cut in half and pits removed (see Note)	6	6
Balsamic vinegar	1/3 cup	75 mL
Liquid honey, warmed	1/4 cup	60 mL
Croissants, cut in half horizontally	3	3
Hard margarine (or butter), melted	2 tbsp.	30 mL
Vanilla ice cream	1 1/2 cups	375 mL
Fresh raspberries	1/2 cup	125 mL

Put peaches into large non-metal bowl. Add vinegar. Toss gently. Cover. Chill for 1 hour, stirring occasionally. Drain and discard liquid.

Preheat barbecue to medium. Cook peaches on greased grill for about 5 minutes per side, brushing with honey, until browned and grill marks appear.

Brush cut sides of croissants with margarine. Cook croissants on greased grill for about 2 minutes per side until crisp and grill marks appear.

Place 1 croissant half, 2 peach halves and 1/4 cup (60 mL) ice cream (about 1 scoop) on each of 6 individual plates.

Sprinkle raspberries over top of each. Serves 6.

1 serving: 338 Calories; 14.9 g Total Fat (5.6 g Mono, 1 g Poly, 7.1 g Sat); 40 mg Cholesterol; 50 g Carbohydrate; 3 g Fibre; 5 g Protein; 323 mg Sodium

Pictured on page 115.

Lemon zest adds a nice balance to sweet grilled cake topped with strawberries and cream. Looks good—tastes heavenly!

Grilled Cake And Strawberries

Maple (or maple-flavoured) syrup	1/2 cup	125 mL
Orange juice	1/3 cup	75 mL
Hard margarine (or butter), melted	2 tbsp.	30 mL
Grated lemon zest	1 tsp.	5 mL
Frozen pound cake, thawed	10 1/2 oz.	298 g
STRAWBERRY TOPPING		
Lemon spread	1/2 cup	125 mL
Whipping cream (or half-and-half cream)	2 tbsp.	30 mL
Halved (or quartered, if large) fresh strawberries	3 cups	750 mL

Combine first 4 ingredients in small bowl.

Remove and discard crust from cake. Cut cake crosswise into 6 equal slices. Cut each slice in half diagonally, for a total of 12 pieces. Dip both sides of each piece into maple syrup mixture. Preheat barbecue to medium. Cook cake on greased grill for about 3 minutes per side until grill marks appear. Place 2 cake slices on each of 6 individual plates.

Strawberry Topping: Heat and stir lemon spread and whipping cream in small saucepan on medium for about 3 minutes until lemon spread is melted. Remove from heat. Let stand for 5 minutes.

Put strawberries into medium bowl. Drizzle with lemon spread mixture. Toss gently. Makes about 3 cups (750 mL) topping. Spoon about 1/2 cup (125 mL) topping over each cake serving. Serves 6.

1 serving: 376 Calories; 15.2 g Total Fat (8.1 g Mono, 1.7 g Poly, 4.4 g Sat); 36 mg Cholesterol; 58 g Carbohydrate; 2 g Fibre; 4 g Protein; 319 mg Sodium

Pictured on page 117.

Top: Chocolate Pizza, page 118
Bottom: Grilled Cake And Strawberries, above

Decadence cloaked in a chocolate cookie crust and creamy, hot fudge topping. Almond liqueur mellows the sweetness of the chocolate.

note

To toast almonds, spread evenly in ungreased shallow pan. Bake in 350°F (175°C) oven for 5 to 10 minutes, stirring or shaking often, until desired doneness.

Chocolate Pizza

Tube of refrigerator chocolate cookie dough	16 oz.	454 g
Granulated sugar	1 tbsp.	15 mL
Ricotta cheese	2 cups	500 mL
Hot fudge ice cream topping	1/4 cup	60 mL
Sour cream	1/4 cup	60 mL
Almond-flavoured liqueur (such as Amaretto)	3 tbsp.	50 mL
Sliced almonds, toasted (see Note)	1/3 cup	75 mL
Hot fudge ice cream topping	2 – 3 tbsp.	30 – 50 mL

Press cookie dough evenly in ungreased 12 inch (30 cm) pizza pan. Sprinkle with sugar. Preheat barbecue to high. Place pan on 1 side of ungreased grill. Turn off burner under pan, turning opposite burner down to medium. Close lid. Cook for about 10 minutes until edge of cookie is just set. Cool.

Beat next 4 ingredients in medium bowl or food processor until smooth. Spread cheese mixture evenly on crust.

Sprinkle with almonds. Drizzle with second amount of ice cream topping. Cuts into 12 wedges.

1 wedge: 327 Calories; 17.2 g Total Fat (7.1 g Mono, 1.7 g Poly, 7.5 g Sat); 34 mg Cholesterol; 35 g Carbohydrate; trace Fibre; 8 g Protein; 133 mg Sodium

Pictured on page 117.

Bananas Caramel

Hard margarine (or butter)	1/2 cup	125 mL
Brown sugar, packed	1/2 cup	125 mL
Sweetened condensed milk	1/2 cup	125 mL
Corn syrup	2 tbsp.	30 mL
Medium bananas, halved lengthwise	4	4
Chopped pecans (or walnuts)	1/3 cup	75 mL

Combine first 4 ingredients in small heavy saucepan. Bring to a boil on medium. Boil, stirring constantly, for 5 minutes. Remove from heat.

Place 2 banana halves on each of 4 individual sheets of heavy-duty (or double layer of regular) foil. Divide and spoon brown sugar mixture evenly over top of each. Fold edges of foil to enclose. Preheat barbecue to medium. Place packets on ungreased grill. Close lid. Cook for 8 to 10 minutes, without turning, until heated through. Transfer bananas to 4 individual plates. Drizzle sauce from foil over each.

Sprinkle each with pecans. Serves 4.

1 serving: 658 Calories; 35.2 g Total Fat (21.1 g Mono, 4.3 g Poly, 7.9 g Sat); 14 mg Cholesterol; 87 g Carbohydrate; 3 g Fibre; 5 g Protein; 359 mg Sodium

Pictured on page 120.

A fantastic dessert that's quick and easy to make for a bunch! Each grilled bite becomes even sweeter with rich caramel sauce.

variation

Cut bananas into 1/2 inch (12 mm) thick slices. Prepare and cook as directed. Serve in 4 individual dessert bowls.

Pictured on page 120.

Photo Legend, next page

1. Grilled Apples, page 122
2. Bananas Caramel, above
3. Barbecued Grapefruit, page 123
4. Grilled Spiced Pineapple, page 122

A simple yet elegant dessert, delicious hot off the grill or made ahead of time and served cold.

note

Omit fresh pineapple slices. Used 12 canned pineapple slices, drained. Cook slices on greased grill for 1 to 2 minutes per side until grill marks appear. Serve with Ricotta Sauce.

Grilled Spiced Pineapple

Maple (or maple-flavoured) syrup	1/2 cup	125 mL
Brandy (or 1/2 tsp., 2 mL, brandy flavouring)	2 tbsp.	30 mL
Ground cinnamon	1/2 tsp.	2 mL
Ground ginger	1/2 tsp.	2 mL
Pepper	1/4 tsp.	1 mL
Slices of fresh pineapple (about 1/2 inch, 12 mm, thick), see Note	6	6
RICOTTA SAUCE		
Ricotta cheese	1 cup	250 mL
Low-fat vanilla yogurt	1/2 cup	125 mL

Combine first 5 ingredients in small bowl. Reserve 2 tbsp. (30 mL) in small cup.

Brush remaining maple syrup mixture evenly over both sides of each pineapple slice. Preheat barbecue to medium. Cook pineapple slices on greased grill for 3 to 5 minutes per side until grill marks appear. Transfer pineapple slices to 6 individual plates.

Ricotta Sauce: Combine ricotta cheese, yogurt and reserved maple syrup mixture in medium bowl. Makes about 1 1/2 cups (375 mL) sauce. Spoon about 1/4 cup (60 mL) sauce into centre of each pineapple slice. Serves 6.

1 serving: 190 Calories; 5.8 g Total Fat (1.6 g Mono, 0.2 g Poly, 3.6 g Sat); 22 mg Cholesterol; 27 g Carbohydrate; 1 g Fibre; 6 g Protein; 55 mg Sodium

Pictured on page 120.

An easy recipe to double or triple for a crowd. Good with or without the raisins. When these are unwrapped, the aroma will have everyone desiring dessert!

Grilled Apples

Medium cooking apples (such as McIntosh), with peel, cores removed	4	4
Brown sugar, packed	1/2 cup	125 mL
Raisins (or currants)	2 tbsp.	30 mL
Ground cinnamon	1/8 tsp.	0.5 mL
Hard margarine (or butter), softened	2 tsp.	10 mL

(continued on next page)

Place 1 apple on each of 4 individual sheets of heavy-duty (or double layer of regular) foil.

Combine brown sugar, raisins and cinnamon in small bowl. Divide and spoon brown sugar mixture into centre of each apple.

Place 1/2 tsp. (2 mL) margarine on top of each. Fold edges of foil to enclose. Preheat barbecue to medium. Place packets on ungreased grill. Close lid. Cook for 15 to 20 minutes, turning occasionally, until apples are softened. Transfer apples to 4 individual plates. Drizzle sauce from foil over each. Serves 4.

1 serving: 222 Calories; 2.5 g Total Fat (1.3 g Mono, 0.3 g Poly, 0.5 g Sat); 0 mg Cholesterol; 53 g Carbohydrate; 3 g Fibre; 0 g Protein; 35 mg Sodium

Pictured on pages 120/121.

Barbecued Grapefruit

Pink medium grapefruit	3	3
Brown sugar, packed	6 tbsp.	100 mL
Dry sherry	6 tbsp.	100 mL
Maraschino cherries, for garnish	6	6

An absolute treat for breakfast or brunch. Use more brown sugar and sherry to make more juices for drizzling if desired. Simply scrumptious!

Cut grapefruit in half crosswise. Remove and discard seeds. Run knife along membranes to loosen fruit segments. Place 1 grapefruit half, cut-side up, on each of 6 individual sheets of heavy-duty (or double layer of regular) foil. Sprinkle each grapefruit half with 1 tbsp. (15 mL) brown sugar and 1 tbsp. (15 mL) sherry. Fold edges of foil to enclose. Preheat barbecue to medium. Place packets on ungreased grill. Close lid. Cook for 10 to 12 minutes until heated through. Transfer grapefruit halves to 6 individual plates.

Garnish each with 1 maraschino cherry. Drizzle with any juices left in foil. Serves 6.

1 serving: 102 Calories; 0.1 g Total Fat (0 g Mono, 0 g Poly, 0 g Sat); 0 mg Cholesterol; 24 g Carbohydrate; 2 g Fibre; 1 g Protein; 6 mg Sodium

Pictured on page 121.

Throughout this book measurements are given in Conventional and Metric measure. To compensate for differences between the two measurements due to rounding, a full metric measure is not always used. The cup used is the standard 8 fluid ounce. Temperature is given in degrees Fahrenheit and Celsius. Baking pan measurements are in inches and centimetres as well as quarts and litres. An exact metric conversion is given on this page as well as the working equivalent (Metric Standard Measure).

Pans

Conventional – Inches	Metric – Centimetres
8 × 8 inch	20 × 20 cm
9 × 9 inch	22 × 22 cm
9 × 13 inch	22 × 33 cm
10 × 15 inch	25 × 38 cm
11 × 17 inch	28 × 43 cm
8 × 2 inch round	20 × 5 cm
9 × 2 inch round	22 × 5 cm
10 × 4 1/2 inch tube	25 × 11 cm
8 × 4 × 3 inch loaf	20 × 10 × 7.5 cm
9 × 5 × 3 inch loaf	22 × 12.5 × 7.5 cm

Oven Temperatures

Fahrenheit (°F)	Celsius (°C)	Fahrenheit (°F)	Celsius (°C)
175°	80°	350°	175°
200°	95°	375°	190°
225°	110°	400°	205°
250°	120°	425°	220°
275°	140°	450°	230°
300°	150°	475°	240°
325°	160°	500°	260°

Spoons

Conventional Measure	Metric Exact Conversion Millilitre (mL)	Metric Standard Measure Millilitre (mL)
1/8 teaspoon (tsp.)	0.6 mL	0.5 mL
1/4 teaspoon (tsp.)	1.2 mL	1 mL
1/2 teaspoon (tsp.)	2.4 mL	2 mL
1 teaspoon (tsp.)	4.7 mL	5 mL
2 teaspoons (tsp.)	9.4 mL	10 mL
1 tablespoon (tbsp.)	14.2 mL	15 mL

Cups

1/4 cup (4 tbsp.)	56.8 mL	60 mL
1/3 cup (5 1/3 tbsp.)	75.6 mL	75 mL
1/2 cup (8 tbsp.)	113.7 mL	125 mL
2/3 cup (10 2/3 tbsp.)	151.2 mL	150 mL
3/4 cup (12 tbsp.)	170.5 mL	175 mL
1 cup (16 tbsp.)	227.3 mL	250 mL
4 1/2 cups	1022.9 mL	1000 mL (1 L)

Dry Measurements

Conventional Measure Ounces (oz.)	Metric Exact Conversion Grams (g)	Metric Standard Measure Grams (g)
1 oz.	28.3 g	28 g
2 oz.	56.7 g	57 g
3 oz.	85.0 g	85 g
4 oz.	113.4 g	125 g
5 oz.	141.7 g	140 g
6 oz.	170.1 g	170 g
7 oz.	198.4 g	200 g
8 oz.	226.8 g	250 g
16 oz.	453.6 g	500 g
32 oz.	907.2 g	1000 g (1 kg)

Casseroles

Canada & Britain		United States	
Standard Size Casserole	Exact Metric Measure	Standard Size Casserole	Exact Metric Measure
1 qt. (5 cups)	1.13 L	1 qt. (4 cups)	900 mL
1 1/2 qts. (7 1/2 cups)	1.69 L	1 1/2 qts. (6 cups)	1.35 L
2 qts. (10 cups)	2.25 L	2 qts. (8 cups)	1.8 L
2 1/2 qts. (12 1/2 cups)	2.81 L	2 1/2 qts. (10 cups)	2.25 L
3 qts. (15 cups)	3.38 L	3 qts. (12 cups)	2.7 L
4 qts. (20 cups)	4.5 L	4 qts. (16 cups)	3.6 L
5 qts. (25 cups)	5.63 L	5 qts. (20 cups)	4.5 L

Most Loved

Most Loved
Salads & Dressings

by Jean Paré

most loved recipe collection

most
loved
salads &
dressings

Pictured on divider:
Mixed Green Salad With Grilled Peppers, page 43

We gratefully acknowledge the following suppliers for their generous support of our
Test and Photography Kitchens:

Broil King Barbecues
Corelle®
Hamilton Beach® Canada
Lagostina®
Proctor Silex® Canada
Tupperware®

Our special thanks to the following businesses for providing props for photography:

Anchor Hocking Canada
Canhome Global
Casa Bugatti
Cherison Enterprises Inc.
Chintz & Company
Danesco Inc.
Emile Henry
Island Pottery Inc.
Klass Works
La Cache
Le Gnome
Linens 'N Things
Mikasa Home Store
Out of the Fire Studio
Pfaltzgraff Canada
Pier 1 Imports
Sears Canada
Stokes
The Bay
The Dazzling Gourmet
Tile Town
Totally Bamboo
Tupperware®
Wal-Mart Canada Inc.
Wiltshire®
Winners
X/S Wares
Zenari's

Pictured from left: Orange Almond Salad, page 39; Summer Fruit Salad, page 78; Martini Dressing, page 108; Warm Chicken Salad, page 46

table of contents

"Never share a recipe you wouldn't use yourself"

the Company's Coming story

Jean Paré (pronounced "jeen PAIR-ee") grew up understanding that the combination of family, friends and home cooking is the best recipe for a good life. From her mother, she learned to appreciate good cooking, while her father praised even her earliest attempts in the kitchen. When Jean left home, she took with her a love of cooking, many family recipes and an intriguing desire to read cookbooks as if they were novels!

When her four children had all reached school age, Jean volunteered to cater the 50th anniversary celebration of the Vermilion School of Agriculture, now Lakeland College, in Alberta, Canada. Working out of her home, Jean prepared a dinner for more than 1,000 people, launching a flourishing catering operation that continued for over 18 years. During that time, she had countless opportunities to test new ideas with immediate feedback—resulting in empty plates and contented customers! Whether preparing cocktail sandwiches for a house party or serving a hot meal for 1,500 people, Jean Paré earned a reputation for great food, courteous service and reasonable prices.

As requests for her recipes increased, Jean was often asked the question, "Why don't you write a cookbook?" Jean responded by teaming up with her son, Grant Lovig, in the fall of 1980 to form Company's Coming Publishing Limited. The publication of *150 Delicious Squares* on April 14, 1981 marked the debut of what would soon become one of the world's most popular cookbook series.

The company has grown since those early days when Jean worked from a spare bedroom in her home. Today, she continues to write recipes while working closely with the staff of the Recipe Factory, as the Company's Coming test kitchen is affectionately known. There she fills the role of mentor, assisting with the development of recipes people most want to use for everyday cooking and easy entertaining. Every Company's Coming recipe is kitchen-tested before it is approved for publication.

Jean's daughter, Gail Lovig, is responsible for marketing and distribution, leading a team that includes sales personnel located in major cities across Canada. Company's Coming cookbooks are distributed in Canada, the United States, Australia and other world markets. Bestsellers many times over in English, Company's Coming cookbooks have also been published in French and Spanish.

Familiar and trusted in home kitchens around the world, Company's Coming cookbooks are offered in a variety of formats. Highly regarded as kitchen workbooks, the softcover Original Series, with its lay-flat plastic comb binding, is still a favourite among readers.

Jean Paré's approach to cooking has always called for quick and easy recipes using everyday ingredients. That view has served her well. The recipient of many awards, including the Queen Elizabeth Golden Jubilee Medal, Jean was appointed Member of the Order of Canada, her country's highest lifetime achievement honour.

Jean continues to gain new supporters by adhering to what she calls The Golden Rule of Cooking: *Never share a recipe you wouldn't use yourself.* It's an approach that has worked—millions of times over!

foreword

For many of us, our first salads were simple mixtures of iceberg lettuce and cucumber, with a few tomato slices for colour. A dollop of bottled dressing finished the dish. It was fast and simple, but hardly the highlight of a meal.

Don't get me wrong; I'm all in favour of simplicity. But when a salad is spectacular, it moves from side-show status to main-stage attraction, and *Most Loved Salads & Dressings* offers everything you need to toss together a show-stopper. How can you miss with a Cranberry Brie or a Bean And Cashew Salad? What about some Minted Pita Chips or Tomato Pesto Croutons tossed on top? *Most Loved Salads & Dressings* invites you to explore the flavours and textures of familiar favourites and some fresh new hits.

Whether it's tossed or molded, marinated or layered, the salads featured here will have friends and family asking for more. Treat them to twists on old themes such as Pesto Pasta and Potato Mint. Rediscover the classics such as Caesar, Greek and Green Goddess, or try new tastes with a Peanut Rice Noodle or Japanese Cabbage Salad. The classics are here too. All-time favourites like Main Macaroni, Overnight Coleslaw and Crispy Cukes await—some things will never go out of style!

Experiment with your favourite greens and dress them for success with delicious homemade dressings such as Blue Cheese, Buttermilk and Italian, or try out-of-the-ordinary mixtures of Apple Spice, Poppy Seed and Creamy Horseradish. Then finish with flair with tasty toppers such as Roasted Pecans or kid-pleasing Little Dilled Snacks.

As our own special topper, all the interesting things we've learned about salads are sprinkled throughout *Most Loved Salads & Dressings*, inviting you to discover the finer points of your favourite salad and dressing ingredients. The possibilities in *Most Loved Salads & Dressings* are endless. Like the other cookbooks in our Most Loved Recipe Collection, it will help you bring exciting colour, flavour and variety to your table.

Jean Paré

nutrition information

Each recipe is analyzed using the most current version of the Canadian Nutrient File from Health Canada, which is based on the United States Department of Agriculture (USDA) Nutrient Database.

- If more than one ingredient is listed (such as "hard margarine or butter"), or if a range is given (1 – 2 tsp., 5 – 10 mL), only the first ingredient or first amount is analyzed.

- For meat, poultry and fish, the serving size per person is based on the recommended 4 oz. (113 g) uncooked weight (without bone), which is 2 – 3 oz. (57 – 85 g) cooked weight (without bone)— approximately the size of a deck of playing cards.

- Milk used is 1% M.F. (milk fat), unless otherwise stated.

- Cooking oil used is canola oil, unless otherwise stated.

- Ingredients indicating "sprinkle," "optional," or "for garnish" are not included in the nutrition information.

Margaret Ng, B.Sc. (Hon.), M.A.
Registered Dietitian

Pictured on page 7.

Julienned meats are a must in a traditional chef's salad. Serve with bread for a satisfying meal.

variation

For individual salads, arrange the lettuce on 6 dinner plates. Scatter the cheese, meats and vegetables over top. Arrange the egg wedges on each plate and drizzle salads with dressing. Serves 6.

tip

To remove the core from a head of iceberg lettuce, hit the core end sharply against the countertop to loosen. The core will then easily twist out.

Chef's Salad

Head of iceberg lettuce, chopped or torn	1	1
Grated medium Cheddar cheese	1 cup	250 mL
Julienned deli chicken (see Note)	1 cup	250 mL
Julienned deli ham	1 cup	250 mL
Sliced celery	1 cup	250 mL
Cold cooked peas	1/2 cup	125 mL
Grated carrot	1/4 cup	60 mL
Cherry tomatoes, halved	12	12
Green onions, sliced	6	6
Large hard-cooked eggs, each cut into 4 wedges	6	6
CHEF'S DRESSING		
Mayonnaise (or salad dressing)	1 cup	250 mL
White vinegar	2 tbsp.	30 mL
Granulated sugar	1 tbsp.	15 mL
Paprika	1 tsp.	5 mL
Salt	1 tsp.	5 mL
Pepper	1/4 tsp.	1 mL

Arrange lettuce on large serving platter.

Scatter next 8 ingredients over top.

Arrange egg wedges around edge of platter.

Chef's Dressing: Combine all 6 ingredients in small bowl. Let stand for 2 to 3 minutes until sugar is dissolved. Stir. Makes about 1 1/3 cups (325 mL) dressing. Drizzle over salad. Serves 6.

1 serving: 568 Calories; 47.8 g Total Fat (23.1 g Mono, 12.1 g Poly, 10.2 g Sat); 296 mg Cholesterol; 10 g Carbohydrate; 2 g Fibre; 25 g Protein; 1169 mg Sodium

Pictured on page 7.

Note: To julienne meat, cut into very thin strips that resemble matchsticks.

A contribution to the salad world from Hollywood, California, that's sure to make you famous with family and friends!

about watercress

Watercress is an aquatic plant with thin, crisp stems and small, glossy, dark green leaves. Its slightly bitter, peppery flavour will put zing in your salads and a delicious accent in your sandwiches. Watercress is available in the produce section of your grocery store. For optimum freshness, place the stems in a glass of water, cover with a plastic bag, and store in the refrigerator for up to 2 days. Be sure to remove the stems and wash the leaves well before using.

Cobb Salad

BLUE COBB DRESSING

Cooking oil	2/3 cup	150 mL
White vinegar	1/3 cup	75 mL
Crumbled blue cheese (about 1 1/4 oz., 35 g)	1/4 cup	60 mL
Dry mustard	1/2 tsp.	2 mL
Granulated sugar	1/2 tsp.	2 mL
Salt	1 tsp.	5 mL
Pepper	1/4 tsp.	1 mL
Garlic powder	1/8 tsp.	0.5 mL
Head of green leaf lettuce, chopped or torn	1	1
Watercress, stems removed, chopped	1 cup	250 mL
Large hard-cooked eggs	3	3
Bacon slices, cooked crisp and crumbled	8	8
Cubed cooked chicken	2 1/2 cups	625 mL
Ripe medium avocado, diced	1	1
Large tomato, finely chopped	1	1
Green onions, sliced	4	4

Blue Cobb Dressing: Combine first 8 ingredients in small bowl (see Note). Makes about 1 1/4 cups (300 mL) dressing.

Put lettuce and watercress into large bowl. Drizzle 1/3 cup (75 mL) dressing over greens. Toss.

Remove yolks from eggs. Chop yolks finely. Grate egg whites.

Put egg yolk, egg white and remaining 5 ingredients in individual piles or rows on top of greens. Serve with remaining dressing. Serves 6.

1 serving: 533 Calories; 44.3 g Total Fat (23.5 g Mono, 10.4 g Poly, 7.3 g Sat); 175 mg Cholesterol; 8 g Carbohydrate; 3 g Fibre; 27 g Protein; 712 mg Sodium

Pictured on page 9.

Note: If preferred, put the blue cheese on top of the greens instead of in the dressing.

*This main dish salad looks lovely
served on a platter, but may also
be arranged in a pretty glass bowl
for an equally attractive presentation.*

making the perfect hard-cooked egg

Follow this simple method to help prevent a grey-green ring from forming around the yolk. Place eggs in a single layer in a saucepan. Add cold water until it's about 1 inch (2.5 cm) above the eggs. Cover. Bring to a boil on high. Remove the saucepan from the heat. Let stand, covered, for 20 minutes. Drain. Cover the eggs with cold water. Change the water each time it warms until the eggs are cool enough to handle. Remove the shells.

Niçoise Salad

Head of iceberg lettuce, chopped or torn	1	1
Head of romaine lettuce, chopped or torn	1	1
Sliced cooked, peeled potato	2 cups	500 mL
Cans of white tuna in water (6 1/2 oz., 184 g, each), drained and broken up	2	2
Can of whole green beans, drained and julienned (see Note)	14 oz.	398 mL
Thinly sliced red onion	1 cup	250 mL
Thinly sliced celery	1 cup	250 mL
Sliced ripe olives	1/2 cup	125 mL
PARSLEY VINAIGRETTE		
Cooking oil	1/2 cup	125 mL
Chopped fresh parsley (or 1 tbsp., 15 mL, flakes)	1/4 cup	60 mL
Red wine vinegar	3 tbsp.	50 mL
Lemon juice	1 tbsp.	15 mL
Salt	1/2 tsp.	2 mL
Pepper	1/4 tsp.	1 mL
Garlic clove, minced (or 1/4 tsp., 1 mL, powder)	1	1
Medium tomatoes, cut into wedges	2	2
Large hard-cooked eggs, quartered	3	3
Anchovies, drained (optional)	6 – 12	6 – 12

Arrange iceberg and romaine lettuce on large serving platter.

Scatter next 6 ingredients over top.

Parsley Vinaigrette: Combine first 7 ingredients in jar with tight-fitting lid. Shake well. Makes about 2/3 cup (150 mL) dressing. Drizzle over salad.

Arrange tomato and egg wedges around edge of platter. Scatter anchovies over top. Serves 6.

1 serving: 385 Calories; 24.8 g Total Fat (13.4 g Mono, 7 g Poly, 2.8 g Sat); 129 mg Cholesterol; 23 g Carbohydrate; 4 g Fibre; 20 g Protein; 599 mg Sodium

Pictured on page 11.

Note: To julienne green beans, cut into very thin strips that resemble matchsticks.

A classic salad that's a meal in itself. For extra flavour, top with a few sardines or anchovies.

Greek Salad

Head of romaine lettuce, chopped or torn	1	1
Head of iceberg lettuce, chopped or torn	1/2	1/2
English cucumber (with peel), cubed	1	1
Medium tomatoes, cubed	2	2
Cubed feta cheese (about 4 oz., 113 g)	3/4 cup	175 mL
Sliced green onion	1/4 cup	60 mL
Sliced ripe olives (see Note)	1/4 cup	60 mL
GREEK DRESSING		
Cooking (or olive) oil	1/2 cup	125 mL
Red wine vinegar	1/4 cup	60 mL
Chopped fresh parsley (or 1 tbsp., 15 mL, flakes)	1/4 cup	60 mL
Salt	1/2 tsp.	2 mL
Pepper	1/8 tsp.	0.5 mL
Dried oregano	1/8 tsp.	0.5 mL
Garlic powder	1/8 tsp.	0.5 mL

Put romaine and iceberg lettuce into large bowl or arrange on large serving platter.

Scatter next 5 ingredients over top.

Greek Dressing: Combine all 7 ingredients in jar with tight-fitting lid. Shake well. Makes about 3/4 cup (175 mL) dressing. Drizzle over salad. Serves 6.

1 serving: 269 Calories; 24.3 g Total Fat (12.5 g Mono, 6.1 g Poly, 4.4 g Sat); 17 mg Cholesterol; 9 g Carbohydrate; 2 g Fibre; 6 g Protein; 468 mg Sodium

Pictured on page 13.

Note: For a more traditional Greek flavour, use Kalamata olives instead of ripe olives.

Crisp spinach, refreshing strawberries and candied pecans—a must-try combination and a proven favourite in the Company's Coming kitchen.

about balsamic vinegar

Traditional balsamic vinegar, made only from grape must, is aged from 12 to more than 30 years in a series of wooden casks, resulting in a sweet, syrupy liquid that's perfect for salad dressings, meat dishes and desserts. A real treat, traditional balsamic vinegar can cost hundreds of dollars for a tiny bottle!

Commercial balsamic vinegar is a combination of grape must and red wine vinegar with added caramel to mimic the sweetness of traditional balsamic. Inexpensive by comparison, it adds a delicious touch to salad dressings and meat dishes. For best flavour, purchase commercial balsamic vinegar with grape must listed first in the label's ingredient list.

Strawberry Pecan Salad

Pecan pieces	2/3 cup	150 mL
Granulated sugar	1/2 cup	125 mL
Water	1/4 cup	60 mL
Fresh spinach, stems removed, lightly packed	6 cups	1.5 L
Sliced fresh strawberries	2 cups	500 mL
Goat (chèvre) cheese, cut up (optional)	3 oz.	85 g
STRAWBERRY DRESSING		
Olive (or cooking) oil	3 tbsp.	50 mL
Strawberry jam, warmed	2 tbsp.	30 mL
Balsamic vinegar	2 tbsp.	30 mL
Pepper	1/8 tsp.	0.5 mL

Spread pecans in single layer in ungreased shallow pan. Bake in 350°F (175°C) oven for 5 to 10 minutes, stirring or shaking often, until toasted.

Heat and stir sugar and water in small saucepan on low until sugar is dissolved. Bring to a boil on medium-high. Boil gently, uncovered, for 5 to 10 minutes, without stirring, until golden brown. Drizzle over pecans. Let stand for about 20 minutes until cool and hard. Chop.

Arrange spinach on 6 salad plates. Scatter pecan mixture, strawberries and cheese over top of each.

Strawberry Dressing: Combine all 4 ingredients in jar with tight-fitting lid. Shake well. Makes about 1/2 cup (125 mL) dressing. Drizzle over each salad. Serves 6.

1 serving: 269 Calories; 16.7 g Total Fat (9.9 g Mono, 4.6 g Poly, 1.3 g Sat); 0 mg Cholesterol; 31 g Carbohydrate; 4 g Fibre; 3 g Protein; 50 mg Sodium

Pictured on page 15 and back cover.

Serve this rich-tasting salad with an omelet or quiche for brunch.

about avocados

When is an avocado ripe? Probably not when you buy it! A ripe avocado will yield to gentle pressure when squeezed, but most avocados available in the grocery store are still hard, indicating, like a green banana, the need to sit on the countertop for a few days to ripen. Putting avocados in a paper bag will speed the ripening process.

Ripe, unpeeled avocados will keep in the refrigerator for up to 2 days. For use in salads, sprinkle avocado with a bit of lemon juice or coat well with dressing to prevent it from darkening when exposed to the air.

Cucumber Avocado Salad

English cucumber (with peel), thinly sliced diagonally	1	1
Red medium pepper, thinly sliced	1	1
Ripe large avocados, sliced	2	2
Smoked salmon, thinly sliced	4 oz.	113 g
CREAMY LEMON DRESSING		
Sour cream	3 tbsp.	50 mL
Water	2 tbsp.	30 mL
Chopped fresh dill (or 3/4 tsp., 4 mL, dill weed)	1 tbsp.	15 mL
Lemon juice	1 tbsp.	15 mL
Salt	1/4 tsp.	1 mL
Finely chopped red onion	1/4 cup	60 mL
Coarsely chopped capers (optional)	1 tbsp.	15 mL
Freshly ground pepper, for garnish		

Layer first 4 ingredients, in order given, on 4 salad plates.

Creamy Lemon Dressing: Combine first 5 ingredients in small bowl. Makes about 1/3 cup (75 mL) dressing. Drizzle over each salad.

Sprinkle each with onion and capers. Garnish with pepper. Serves 4.

1 serving: 239 Calories; 18.4 g Total Fat (10.7 g Mono, 2.4 g Poly, 3.7 g Sat); 11 mg Cholesterol; 14 g Carbohydrate; 4 g Fibre; 9 g Protein; 388 mg Sodium

Pictured on page 19.

An attractive salad with vibrant summer colours and a fresh-tasting dressing.

Papaya And Mixed Greens

Mixed salad greens, lightly packed	4 cups	1 L
Medium papaya, seeds reserved, cubed	1	1
Medium tomatoes, seeds removed, cubed	2	2
Chopped green onion	1/4 cup	60 mL

(continued on next page)

MUSTARD DRESSING

Peanut (or cooking) oil	3 tbsp.	50 mL
White wine vinegar	2 tbsp.	30 mL
Reserved papaya seeds	2 tbsp.	30 mL
Liquid honey	1 tbsp.	15 mL
Dry mustard	1 tsp.	5 mL
Salt	1/4 tsp.	1 mL
Pepper, sprinkle		

Arrange salad greens on 6 salad plates.

Scatter papaya, tomato and onion over top of each.

Mustard Dressing: Combine all 7 ingredients in jar with tight-fitting lid. Shake well. Makes about 1/2 cup (125 mL) dressing. Drizzle over each salad. Serves 6.

1 serving: 111 Calories; 7.3 g Total Fat (3.3 g Mono, 2.4 g Poly, 1.2 g Sat); 0 mg Cholesterol; 12 g Carbohydrate; 2 g Fibre; 2 g Protein; 114 mg Sodium

Pictured below.

about mixed salad greens

Mixed salad greens are also known as "mesclun" and are available in bags and bulk in the produce section of your grocery store. This mix of small young greens often includes arugula, curly endive, mizuna, oak leaf, radicchio or sorrel. You can make your own mesclun by combining your favourite types of lettuce with other salad greens.

A layered salad with a novel presentation. These can be made earlier in the day and chilled until serving time.

storing celery

For optimum freshness, store celery in the refrigerator in a perforated plastic bag or in an airtight container equipped with a drip tray. Either container will help keep condensation away from the celery, allowing for a longer shelf life than plastic alone.

Parfait Crab Salad

Large hard-cooked eggs, chopped	2	2
Can of crabmeat (or imitation), drained, cartilage removed, flaked	4 1/4 oz.	120 g
Salad dressing (or mayonnaise)	1/4 cup	60 mL
Sour cream	3 tbsp.	50 mL
Chopped fresh parsley (or 1 tsp., 5 mL, flakes)	1 1/2 tbsp.	25 mL
Milk	1 tbsp.	15 mL
Sweet pickle relish	2 tsp.	10 mL
Finely chopped celery	2 tsp.	10 mL
Salt	1/4 tsp.	1 mL
Onion powder	1/8 tsp.	0.5 mL
Chopped or torn iceberg lettuce, lightly packed	1 cup	250 mL
Green onions, thinly sliced	2	2
Cold cooked peas	1/2 cup	125 mL
Grated medium Cheddar cheese	1/4 cup	60 mL

Combine first 10 ingredients in medium bowl.

Put lettuce into 4 stemmed large parfait glasses (see Note).

Spoon crabmeat mixture on top of lettuce. Layer onion and peas on top of crabmeat mixture.

Sprinkle each with cheese. Chill. Serves 4.

1 serving: 208 Calories; 14.7 g Total Fat (6.4 g Mono, 3.1 g Poly, 4 g Sat); 124 mg Cholesterol; 8 g Carbohydrate; 1 g Fibre; 11 g Protein; 567 mg Sodium

Pictured on page 19.

Note: If you don't have parfait glasses, large wine glasses or water goblets work equally well.

Top: Parfait Crab Salad, above
Bottom: Cucumber Avocado Salad, page 16

The perfect salad for company! Make it the day before if you like. Just cover it with plastic wrap and chill until ready to serve.

tip

It's always nice to have bacon on hand to add smoky flavour to greens. For ease and convenience, store cooked bacon strips in an airtight container in the freezer. Simply remove as many strips as you need to crumble into salads.

Multi-Layered Salad

Head of iceberg lettuce (see Note), chopped or torn	1	1
Sliced celery	1 cup	250 mL
Large hard-cooked eggs, chopped or sliced	6	6
Cold cooked (or frozen, thawed) peas	1 cup	250 mL
Chopped green pepper	1/2 cup	125 mL
Green onions, sliced	8	8
Can of sliced water chestnuts, drained	8 oz.	227 mL
Bacon slices, cooked crisp and crumbled	8	8
SOUR CREAM DRESSING		
Sour cream	1 cup	250 mL
Salad dressing (or mayonnaise)	1 cup	250 mL
Granulated sugar	2 tbsp.	30 mL
Grated medium Cheddar cheese	1 cup	250 mL
Bacon slices, cooked crisp and crumbled	4	4

Arrange lettuce in bottom of 3 quart (3 L) glass baking dish or large glass bowl.

Layer next 7 ingredients, in order given, on top of lettuce.

Sour Cream Dressing: Combine sour cream, salad dressing and sugar in small bowl. Makes about 2 cups (500 mL) dressing. Spoon on top of salad. Carefully spread dressing to edge of baking dish to seal.

Scatter cheese over dressing. Scatter second amount of bacon over top. Serves 10.

1 serving: 344 Calories; 26.6 g Total Fat (11.9 g Mono, 5.3 g Poly, 7.9 g Sat); 164 mg Cholesterol; 14 g Carbohydrate; 1 g Fibre; 12 g Protein; 431 mg Sodium

Pictured on page 21.

Note: For a more colourful and nutritious salad, use a mixture of iceberg and romaine lettuce plus some spinach leaves.

This large, beautiful salad may be made up to two days ahead. Your guests will love the delicious Mexican flavours and the crunchy texture.

Rio Ranchero Layered Salad

Chopped or torn romaine lettuce, lightly packed	8 cups	2 L
Large hard-cooked eggs, sliced	8	8
Halved cherry tomatoes	3 cups	750 mL
Can of black beans, rinsed and drained	19 oz.	540 mL
Green onions, sliced	4	4
Thinly sliced celery	1/2 cup	125 mL
Green medium pepper, diced	1	1
Cans of kernel corn (7 oz., 199 mL, each), drained	2	2
Ripe large avocados, cubed	2	2
Lime juice	1 tbsp.	15 mL
SASSY SALSA DRESSING		
Mayonnaise (or salad dressing)	1 cup	250 mL
Sour cream	1 cup	250 mL
Chunky salsa	2/3 cup	150 mL
Finely chopped fresh parsley (or 2 tbsp., 30 mL, flakes)	1/2 cup	125 mL
Lime juice	1/3 cup	75 mL
Grated lime zest	1/2 tsp.	2 mL
Ground cumin	1/2 tsp.	2 mL
Chili powder	1/2 tsp.	2 mL
Granulated sugar	1/2 tsp.	2 mL
Cherry tomatoes	8	8
Grated sharp Cheddar cheese	3/4 cup	175 mL
Grated Monterey Jack With Jalapeño cheese	3/4 cup	175 mL
Bacon slices, cooked crisp and crumbled (optional)	8	8
Sliced ripe olives	2 tbsp.	30 mL
Diced jalapeño pepper (see Tip)	2 tbsp.	30 mL

(continued on next page)

Put lettuce into extra-large glass bowl. Pack down slightly.

Press some egg slices against inside of bowl to decorate (see photo, page 25). Arrange remaining egg slices in single layer on top of lettuce.

Arrange some tomato halves, cut-side out, against inside of bowl to decorate. Layer remaining tomato halves on top of egg slices and lettuce.

Layer next 5 ingredients, in order given, on top of tomato halves.

Put avocado into small bowl. Drizzle with lime juice. Toss gently until coated. Scatter on top of corn.

Sassy Salsa Dressing: Combine first 9 ingredients in medium bowl. Makes about 3 cups (750 mL) dressing. Spoon on top of avocado. Carefully spread dressing to edge of bowl to seal. Cover with plastic wrap. Chill.

Just before serving, scatter remaining 6 ingredients, in order given, over dressing. Serves 12.

1 serving: 424 Calories; 33.5 g Total Fat (16.2 g Mono, 6.9 g Poly, 8.4 g Sat); 178 mg Cholesterol; 20 g Carbohydrate; 4 g Fibre; 13 g Protein; 430 mg Sodium

Pictured on page 25.

about romaine lettuce

The slightly bitter flavour of these long leaves has made romaine lettuce a popular choice for Caesar salads. But don't let that limit you. Romaine is wonderful used alone, or in combination with other greens, in any leafy salad. For optimum freshness, wrap washed leaves loosely with damp paper towels and put in a plastic bag, or place washed leaves in an airtight container equipped with a drip tray. Store in the refrigerator for up to 5 days.

This salad takes a little more time to prepare, but it's worth it! Fresh corn kernels and roasted peppers liven up crisp greens and add a hint of sweetness to the salad.

about corn on the cob

For maximum flavour and freshness, corn is best eaten the same day it's purchased; even better, the same day it's picked! If that's not convenient, corn may be stored in its husk in the refrigerator. Keep in mind that the longer corn is off the stalk before cooking, the more of its natural sugar will convert to starch, causing gradual lessening of its sweet flavour.

When buying corn, look for cobs with dark green husks and golden brown silk. Although tempting, removing the husks in the grocery store will speed moisture loss from the kernels and should be avoided. Instead, choose ears that have full, rounded tips, indicating that the cobs are mature.

Corn And Tomato Salad

Medium corncobs	2	2
Boiling water		
Green medium peppers, quartered	2	2
Head of romaine lettuce, chopped or torn	1	1
Halved cherry tomatoes	2 cups	500 mL
Thinly sliced red onion	3/4 cup	175 mL
Chopped fresh mint leaves (or 1 tbsp., 15 mL, dried)	1/4 cup	60 mL
SWEET CHILI DRESSING		
Olive (or cooking) oil	1/4 cup	60 mL
Sweet chili sauce	3 tbsp.	50 mL
White wine vinegar	2 tbsp.	30 mL
Garlic clove, minced (or 1/4 tsp., 1 mL, powder)	1	1
Salt	1/4 tsp.	1 mL

Cook corncobs in boiling water in large pot or Dutch oven for 5 to 7 minutes until tender-crisp. Drain. Cool. Cut corn kernels into 2 inch (5 cm) long strips from each cob. Put into large bowl.

Arrange green pepper pieces, skin-side up, on ungreased baking sheet. Broil on top rack in oven for 10 to 15 minutes until skins are blistered and blackened. Transfer to small bowl. Cover with plastic wrap. Let sweat for about 15 minutes until cool enough to handle. Peel and discard skins. Cut into 2 inch (5 cm) strips. Add to corn.

Add next 4 ingredients. Toss gently.

Sweet Chili Dressing: Combine all 5 ingredients in jar with tight-fitting lid. Shake well. Makes about 2/3 cup (150 mL) dressing. Drizzle over salad. Toss gently. Serves 8.

1 serving: 136 Calories; 7.9 g Total Fat (5.5 g Mono, 0.9 g Poly, 1.1 g Sat); 0 mg Cholesterol; 16 g Carbohydrate; 4 g Fibre; 3 g Protein; 174 mg Sodium

Pictured on page 25.

Top Left: Rio Ranchero Layered Salad, page 22
Bottom Right: Corn And Tomato Salad, above

Spinach salad with a lemon twist. You'll love the tangy dressing!

about spinach

Spinach is available in bags or bunches in the produce section of your grocery store. Store spinach bunches in a perforated plastic bag in the refrigerator for up to 5 days. Wash leaves thoroughly just before using. Although certainly edible, removing the stems will make spinach more attractive for use in salads.

A bountiful salad with a tasty dressing. Sure to please everyone.

Spinach Mushroom Salad

Sliced fresh white mushrooms	2 cups	500 mL
Bag of fresh spinach, stems removed	10 oz.	284 g
Bacon slices, cooked crisp and crumbled	6	6
Sliced green onion	1/3 cup	75 mL
LIGHT LEMON DRESSING		
Egg yolk (large), see Note	1	1
Cooking oil	2 tbsp.	30 mL
Lemon juice	2 tbsp.	30 mL
Granulated sugar	1/2 tsp.	2 mL
Salt	3/4 tsp.	4 mL
Pepper	1/8 tsp.	0.5 mL

Put first 4 ingredients into large bowl. Toss.

Light Lemon Dressing: Whisk all 6 ingredients in small bowl. Makes about 1/3 cup (75 mL) dressing. Drizzle over salad. Toss well. Serves 8.

1 serving: 81 Calories; 6.7 g Total Fat (3.4 g Mono, 1.5 g Poly, 1.3 g Sat); 31 mg Cholesterol; 3 g Carbohydrate; 1 g Fibre; 3 g Protein; 329 mg Sodium

Pictured on page 27.

Note: Immediately following preparation, salad dressings containing uncooked eggs should be placed in the refrigerator and stored there until serving time.

Tossed Salad

Head of iceberg lettuce, chopped or torn	1	1
Large hard-cooked eggs, chopped	2	2
Sliced fresh white mushrooms	1 cup	250 mL
Chopped English cucumber (with peel)	1/2 cup	125 mL
Sliced celery	1/2 cup	125 mL
Medium tomato, chopped	1	1
Green onions, sliced	4	4
Radishes, sliced	6	6

(continued on next page)

SIMPLE MAYONNAISE DRESSING

Mayonnaise (or salad dressing)	1/2 cup	125 mL
Milk	2 tbsp.	30 mL
Prepared mustard	1 tsp.	5 mL
Granulated sugar	1 tsp.	5 mL

Put first 8 ingredients into large bowl. Toss.

Simple Mayonnaise Dressing: Combine all 4 ingredients in small bowl. Makes about 2/3 cup (150 mL) dressing. Drizzle over salad. Toss well. Serves 8.

1 serving: 148 Calories; 13.4 g Total Fat (7 g Mono, 4.2 g Poly, 1.6 g Sat); 63 mg Cholesterol; 4 g Carbohydrate; 1 g Fibre; 3 g Protein; 119 mg Sodium

Pictured below.

Top: Spinach Mushroom Salad, page 26
Centre Right and Bottom: Tossed Salad, page 26

A salad that's stood the test of time!

caesar croutons

Heat 2 tbsp. (30 mL) olive (or cooking) oil in a large frying pan on medium. Add 2 cups (500 mL) dry white bread cubes. Sprinkle with garlic salt (for Secret Caesar, omit garlic salt). Heat and stir for about 3 minutes until golden. Remove the croutons to a paper towel-lined plate. Cool.

Caesar Salad

Head of romaine lettuce, chopped or torn	1	1
Grated Parmesan cheese	1/2 cup	125 mL
Caesar Croutons (recipe, left)		

EASY CAESAR DRESSING

Mayonnaise (or salad dressing)	1 cup	250 mL
Lemon juice	1 tbsp.	15 mL
Worcestershire sauce	1/2 tsp.	2 mL
Garlic clove, minced (or 1/4 tsp., 1 mL, powder)	1	1
Salt	1/4 tsp.	1 mL
Pepper	1/8 tsp.	0.5 mL

Put lettuce, Parmesan cheese and croutons into large bowl. Toss.

Easy Caesar Dressing: Combine all 6 ingredients in small bowl. Makes about 1 cup (250 mL) dressing. Drizzle over salad. Toss well. Serves 6.

1 serving: 401 Calories; 36.5 g Total Fat (19.4 g Mono, 10.9 g Poly, 5.4 g Sat); 30 mg Cholesterol; 12 g Carbohydrate; 2 g Fibre; 7 g Protein; 649 mg Sodium

Pictured on page 29.

When you crave Caesar Salad, but don't care for the strong flavour of fresh garlic, this one's for you. Jean's secret for a more subtle taste is to use garlic powder instead.

variation

For extra good taste, add 1/2 cup (125 mL) crumbled blue cheese to your favourite Caesar salad.

Secret Caesar

Head of romaine lettuce, chopped or torn	1	1
Grated Parmesan cheese	1/4 cup	60 mL
Caesar Croutons (recipe, above left)		

SECRET CAESAR DRESSING

Egg yolk (large), see Note	1	1
Grated Parmesan cheese	1/2 cup	125 mL
Cooking oil	6 tbsp.	100 mL
Red wine vinegar	2 tbsp.	30 mL
Lemon juice	1 tbsp.	15 mL
Worcestershire sauce	1 tsp.	5 mL
Garlic powder	1/4 tsp.	1 mL
Salt	1/4 tsp.	1 mL
Pepper	1/8 tsp.	0.5 mL

(continued on next page)

Put lettuce, Parmesan cheese and croutons into large bowl. Toss.

Secret Caesar Dressing: Whisk all 9 ingredients in small bowl. Makes about 3/4 cup (175 mL) dressing. Drizzle over salad. Toss well. Serves 6.

1 serving: 271 Calories; 21.4 g Total Fat (11 g Mono, 4.7 g Poly, 4.5 g Sat); 47 mg Cholesterol; 12 g Carbohydrate; 2 g Fibre; 9 g Protein; 537 mg Sodium

Pictured below.

Note: Immediately following preparation, salad dressings containing uncooked eggs should be placed in the refrigerator and stored there until serving time.

Top right: Caesar Salad, page 28
Bottom Right and Left: Secret Caesar, page 28

Spicy chicken takes this Caesar from a side to a complete meal.

about "blackened" cooking

"Blackened" cooking originated in New Orleans. Traditionally, meat or fish is rubbed with Cajun spices and then cooked quickly in a hot, greased pan, giving the meat a crispy, dark-coloured crust. In this recipe we've added the spices during cooking to speed preparation, with equally tasty results.

tip

Red and white wine vinegars may be used interchangeably in most salad dressings. A recipe may call for one over the other because each offers a slightly different flavour and colour, much the same as red and white wines. However, as each offers an agreeable tang, feel free to use whichever you have on hand.

Blackened Chicken Caesar Salad

CREAMY CAESAR DRESSING

Grated Parmesan cheese	1/2 cup	125 mL
Cooking oil	3 tbsp.	50 mL
Sour cream	3 tbsp.	50 mL
White (or red) wine vinegar	1 tbsp.	15 mL
Lemon juice	1 tsp.	5 mL
Worcestershire sauce	1 tsp.	5 mL
Garlic salt	1/2 tsp.	2 mL
Pepper	1/4 tsp.	1 mL

BLACKENED CHICKEN

Cooking oil	1 tbsp.	15 mL
Boneless, skinless chicken breast halves, cut into 3/4 inch (2 cm) pieces	2 lbs.	900 g
Ketchup	2 tbsp.	30 mL
Paprika	1 tbsp.	15 mL
Salt	2 tsp.	10 mL
Pepper	1/2 tsp.	2 mL
Onion powder	1/2 tsp.	2 mL
Ground thyme	1/2 tsp.	2 mL
Chili powder	1/2 tsp.	2 mL
Cayenne pepper	1/2 tsp.	2 mL
Heads of romaine lettuce, chopped or torn	2	2
Croutons	1 cup	250 mL
Grated Parmesan cheese	1/4 cup	60 mL

Grated Parmesan cheese, for garnish

Creamy Caesar Dressing: Combine first 8 ingredients in small bowl. Makes about 1/2 cup (125 mL) dressing. Chill for 10 minutes to blend flavours.

Blackened Chicken: Heat wok or large frying pan on medium-high until very hot. Add cooking oil. Add chicken. Stir-fry for 6 to 7 minutes until chicken turns white.

(continued on next page)

Add next 8 ingredients. Stir-fry for 8 to 10 minutes until chicken is no longer pink inside. Remove from heat.

Put lettuce, croutons and second amount of Parmesan cheese into large bowl. Toss. Drizzle dressing over salad. Toss. Arrange on 8 dinner plates. Scatter chicken mixture over top of each.

Garnish each with Parmesan cheese. Serves 8.

1 serving: 290 Calories; 13.9 g Total Fat (6.2 g Mono, 2.9 g Poly, 3.7 g Sat); 75 mg Cholesterol; 9 g Carbohydrate; 2 g Fibre; 32 g Protein; 983 mg Sodium

Pictured below.

This main course salad is a treat served in Tortilla Bowls. If you're strapped for time, toss the salad with broken-up tortilla chips and serve individual portions on brightly coloured plates.

tortilla bowls

Grease the bottom and outside of an ovenproof 2 cup (500 mL) liquid measure. Invert onto a baking sheet. Press a 7 1/2 inch (19 cm) diameter flour tortilla over the bottom and side of the liquid measure. Bake in a 325°F (160°C) oven for 7 to 10 minutes, pressing the tortilla against the measure occasionally, until brown spots appear. Makes 1 tortilla bowl.

Pictured on page 33.

Mexican Salad

Cooking oil	1 tsp.	5 mL
Lean ground beef	1/2 lb.	225 g
Water	1/2 cup	125 mL
Taco seasoning mix, stir before measuring	4 tsp.	20 mL
Shredded iceberg lettuce, lightly packed	4 cups	1 L
Can of pinto beans, rinsed and drained	19 oz.	540 mL
Medium tomato, diced	1	1
Small red pepper, diced	1	1
Very thinly sliced red onion	1 cup	250 mL
Tortilla Bowls (recipe, left)	6	6
CHILI DRESSING		
Plain yogurt	1/2 cup	125 mL
Light sour cream	1/2 cup	125 mL
Chili sauce	3 tbsp.	50 mL
Onion powder	1/2 tsp.	2 mL
Salt	1/4 tsp.	1 mL
Garlic powder	1/8 tsp.	0.5 mL

Heat cooking oil in medium frying pan on medium. Add ground beef. Scramble-fry for about 10 minutes until no longer pink. Drain.

Add water and taco seasoning. Stir. Reduce heat to medium-low. Cook, uncovered, for about 5 minutes, stirring occasionally, until liquid is evaporated. Cool. Transfer to large bowl.

Add next 5 ingredients. Toss.

Spoon salad into Tortilla Bowls.

Chili Dressing: Combine all 6 ingredients in small bowl. Makes about 1 1/4 cups (300 mL) dressing. Drizzle over each salad. Serves 6.

1 serving: 243 Calories; 6.9 g Total Fat (3 g Mono, 0.9 g Poly, 3.4 g Sat); 25 mg Cholesterol; 32 g Carbohydrate; 6 g Fibre; 15 g Protein; 613 mg Sodium

Pictured on page 33.

A great addition to any meal. Easy to double for a large crowd.

about iceberg lettuce

Originally called "crisphead," this popular lettuce became known as "iceberg" in the days before modern refrigeration, when shipping boxes were covered with ice to keep the lettuce fresh during transportation. It is also known as "head lettuce" because it grows in round, tightly packed heads. It can be chopped, torn, shredded or cut into wedges, making it one of the most versatile salad greens available. To store, put whole iceberg lettuce in a plastic bag or other airtight container and keep in the refrigerator for up to 2 weeks.

Green Goddess Salad

Head of iceberg lettuce, chopped or torn	1	1
Canned crabmeat (or salad shrimp)	1/2 cup	125 mL
GREEN GODDESS DRESSING		
Salad dressing (or mayonnaise)	1/2 cup	125 mL
Sour cream	1/4 cup	60 mL
Chopped green onion	2 tbsp.	30 mL
Chopped fresh parsley (or 1 1/2 tsp., 7 mL, flakes)	2 tbsp.	30 mL
Anchovy paste	1 tsp.	5 mL
Worcestershire sauce	1/2 tsp.	2 mL
Prepared mustard	1/4 tsp.	1 mL
Garlic powder	1/8 tsp.	0.5 mL
Salt	1/4 tsp.	1 mL
Pepper, sprinkle		

Put lettuce and crabmeat into large bowl. Toss.

Green Goddess Dressing: Combine all 10 ingredients in small bowl. Makes about 1 cup (250 mL) dressing. Drizzle over salad. Toss well. Serves 8 to 10.

1 serving: 110 Calories; 9 g Total Fat (4.6 g Mono, 2.7 g Poly, 1.3 g Sat); 13 mg Cholesterol; 4 g Carbohydrate; 0 g Fibre; 3 g Protein; 274 mg Sodium

Pictured on page 35.

The sweet, smoky dressing tastes so good on simple romaine lettuce. Make the dressing just before serving so that it's still warm.

Warm Bacon Lettuce Salad

Head of romaine lettuce, chopped or torn	1	1
Green onions, chopped	3	3
WARM BACON DRESSING		
Apple cider vinegar	1/4 cup	60 mL
Granulated sugar	2 tbsp.	30 mL
Water	2 tbsp.	30 mL
Salt	1/2 tsp.	2 mL
Pepper	1/4 tsp.	1 mL

(continued on next page)

Bacon slices, diced	5	5
Chopped onion	1/2 cup	125 mL
Large hard-cooked egg, chopped	1	1

Put lettuce and green onion into large bowl. Toss.

Warm Bacon Dressing: Combine first 5 ingredients in jar with tight-fitting lid. Shake well.

Cook bacon and onion in medium frying pan until bacon is almost crisp. Add bacon, onion and drippings to vinegar mixture. Shake well. Makes about 1/2 cup (125 mL) dressing. Drizzle over salad. Toss well.

Sprinkle with egg. Serve immediately. Serves 4.

1 serving: 117 Calories; 5.5 g Total Fat (2.4 g Mono, 0.8 g Poly, 1.8 g Sat); 61 mg Cholesterol; 12 g Carbohydrate; 2 g Fibre; 6 g Protein; 448 mg Sodium

Pictured below.

Top: Green Goddess Salad, page 34
Bottom: Warm Bacon Lettuce Salad, page 34

An inviting summer salad with a light, sweet and sour flavour. Almonds add a perfectly nutty touch.

segmenting oranges

Cut a small slice of peel from both ends so that the flesh is exposed. Place the orange, cut-side down, on a cutting board. Remove the peel with a sharp knife, cutting down and around the flesh, leaving as little pith as possible (photo 1). Over a small bowl, cut on either side of the membranes to release the segments (photo 2).

Fruity Butter Lettuce Salad

Head of butter lettuce, chopped or torn	1	1
Medium oranges, peeled and segmented	2	2
Sliced fresh strawberries	2/3 cup	150 mL
Crumbled feta cheese (about 2 1/2 oz., 70 g)	1/2 cup	125 mL
Sliced almonds, toasted (see Tip)	1/2 cup	125 mL
ORANGE DRESSING		
Olive (or cooking) oil	2 tbsp.	30 mL
Orange juice	2 tbsp.	30 mL
White wine vinegar	1 tbsp.	15 mL
Granulated sugar	2 tsp.	10 mL
Sesame oil, for flavour	1/4 tsp.	1 mL
Salt	1/4 tsp.	1 mL
Pepper, just a pinch		

Put first 5 ingredients into large bowl. Toss gently.

Orange Dressing: Combine all 7 ingredients in jar with tight-fitting lid. Shake well. Makes about 1/3 cup (75 mL) dressing. Drizzle over salad. Toss gently. Serves 6.

1 serving: 171 Calories; 12.7 g Total Fat (7.3 g Mono, 1.7 g Poly, 3.2 g Sat); 12 mg Cholesterol; 12 g Carbohydrate; 3 g Fibre; 5 g Protein; 254 mg Sodium

Pictured on page 37.

Top: Spinach Squash Salad, page 38
Bottom: Fruity Butter Lettuce Salad, page 36

An aromatic salad with rich, autumn colours and a delicate, nutty flavour.

tip

Always dry salad greens thoroughly after washing so that excess water does not dilute the dressing or prevent it from coating the salad.

about butternut squash

A long, straight neck and round bottom give butternut squash its distinct appearance. Its cream-coloured peel is easy to remove, revealing a deep orange flesh. Grilled, baked or steamed, butternut squash adds a sweet, nutty flavour to salads, soups, stews and desserts.

Spinach Squash Salad

Small butternut squash, peeled and cut into 1/8 inch (3 mm) slices	1/2	1/2
Fresh white medium mushrooms, halved	12	12
Thin prosciutto (or back bacon) slices, cooked crisp and broken into 3/4 inch (2 cm) pieces	6	6
Bag of fresh spinach, stems removed	10 oz.	284 g
Shaved Parmesan cheese	1/2 cup	125 mL
APPLE SPICE DRESSING		
Olive (or cooking) oil	1/4 cup	60 mL
Apple cider vinegar	2 tbsp.	30 mL
Garlic clove, minced (or 1/4 tsp., 1 mL, powder)	1	1
Ground nutmeg	1/8 tsp.	0.5 mL
Ground cinnamon	1/8 tsp.	0.5 mL
Salt	1/8 tsp.	0.5 mL
Pepper	1/8 tsp.	0.5 mL

Spray both sides of each squash slice with cooking spray. Preheat electric grill for 5 minutes or gas barbecue to medium (to broil vegetables, see page 42). Cook squash on greased grill for about 5 minutes per side until browned and tender. Transfer to large plate. Cut into 3/4 inch (2 cm) pieces. Put into large bowl.

Spray mushroom halves with cooking spray. Cook on greased grill for about 5 minutes, turning once, until browned. Transfer to large plate. Cut each half into 2 pieces. Add to squash.

Add prosciutto, spinach and Parmesan cheese. Toss gently.

Apple Spice Dressing: Combine all 7 ingredients in jar with tight-fitting lid. Shake well. Makes about 1/3 cup (75 mL) dressing. Drizzle over salad. Toss gently. Serves 4.

1 serving: 307 Calories; 23.6 g Total Fat (14 g Mono, 2.1 g Poly, 6.2 g Sat); 18 mg Cholesterol; 15 g Carbohydrate; 4 g Fibre; 12 g Protein; 536 mg Sodium

Pictured on page 37.

Orange Almond Salad

Head of romaine lettuce, chopped or torn	1	1
Can of mandarin orange segments, drained	10 oz.	284 mL
Slivered almonds, toasted (see Tip)	1/4 cup	60 mL
Green onions, sliced	2	2
SWEET VINAIGRETTE		
Cooking oil	1/4 cup	60 mL
White vinegar	1/4 cup	60 mL
Granulated sugar	1/4 cup	60 mL

Simply delicious. Mandarin oranges add a refreshing flavour to this light salad.

tip

To toast almonds, spread them in a single layer in an ungreased shallow pan. Bake in a 350°F (175°C) oven for 5 to 10 minutes, stirring or shaking often, until desired doneness.

Put first 4 ingredients into large bowl. Toss gently.

Sweet Vinaigrette: Combine olive oil, vinegar and sugar in jar with tight-fitting lid. Shake well. Makes about 1/2 cup (125 mL) vinaigrette. Drizzle over salad. Toss gently. Serves 4.

1 serving: 268 Calories; 19.3 g Total Fat (11.5 g Mono, 5.4 g Poly, 1.5 g Sat); 0 mg Cholesterol; 23 g Carbohydrate; 3 g Fibre; 4 g Protein; 10 mg Sodium

Pictured below.

This large salad is perfect for a buffet or summertime barbecue. The savoury dressing has a flavour that is unsurpassed!

about anchovy paste

Anchovy paste is a mixture of crushed anchovies, vinegar, water and spices, and comes in a tube for easy use. Canned anchovies may be mashed with a little bit of the oil from the can for an acceptable substitute.

Chunky Vegetable Salad

SWEET VEGGIE DRESSING

Olive (or cooking) oil	1/3 cup	75 mL
Coarsely chopped onion	1/4 cup	60 mL
Coarsely chopped carrot	1/4 cup	60 mL
Large egg (see Note)	1	1
White wine vinegar	2 tbsp.	30 mL
Granulated sugar	1 tbsp.	15 mL
Garlic cloves, minced (or 1/2 – 3/4 tsp., 2 – 4 mL, powder)	2 – 3	2 – 3
Anchovy paste	2 – 3 tsp.	10 – 15 mL
Dried oregano	1/2 tsp.	2 mL
Paprika	1/2 tsp.	2 mL
Celery seed	1/4 tsp.	1 mL
Salt	1/4 tsp.	1 mL
Pepper	1/8 tsp.	0.5 mL
Capers (optional)	1 tsp.	5 mL
English cucumber (with peel), cubed	1	1
Green medium pepper, cut into 3/4 inch (2 cm) pieces	1	1
Yellow medium pepper, cut into 3/4 inch (2 cm) pieces	1	1
Medium tomatoes, seeds removed, cubed	2	2
Coarsely chopped iceberg lettuce, lightly packed	6 cups	1.5 L
Crumbled feta cheese (about 3 oz., 85 g), optional	2/3 cup	150 mL

Sweet Veggie Dressing: Process first 14 ingredients in blender or food processor for about 2 minutes until smooth. Chill for 30 minutes to blend flavours. Makes about 1 cup (250 mL) dressing.

Put next 4 ingredients into large bowl. Drizzle with dressing. Toss.

(continued on next page)

Add lettuce and cheese. Toss gently. Serves 8.

1 serving: *139 Calories; 10.7 g Total Fat (7.3 g Mono, 1.1 g Poly, 1.6 g Sat); 28 mg Cholesterol; 10 g Carbohydrate; 2 g Fibre; 3 g Protein; 159 mg Sodium*

Pictured below.

Note: Immediately following preparation, salad dressings containing uncooked eggs should be placed in the refrigerator and stored there until serving time.

Clockwise from Top Left:
Grilled Veggie Salad, page 42
Chunky Vegetable Salad, page 40
Apple And Shrimp Salad, page 44

A bright, colourful salad that's sure to become a favourite! The grilled vegetable portion of this salad may be prepared a day ahead and chilled overnight.

broiling peppers

Peppers may be broiled in the oven instead of grilled. Place cut peppers, skin-side up, on a greased broiler pan. Broil on the top rack for 10 to 15 minutes until skins are blistered and blackened. Transfer to a small bowl. Cover with plastic wrap. Let sweat for about 15 minutes until cool enough to handle. Peel and discard skins.

broiling vegetables

Vegetables may be broiled in the oven instead of grilled. Place vegetables on a greased broiler pan. Broil on the top rack and turn occasionally, until desired doneness.

Grilled Veggie Salad

Red medium pepper, quartered	1	1
Medium zucchini (with peel), cut lengthwise into 1/4 inch (6 mm) slices	1	1
Thinly sliced peeled yam (or sweet potato)	1 cup	250 mL
BALSAMIC DRESSING		
Olive (or cooking) oil	3 tbsp.	50 mL
Balsamic vinegar	2 tbsp.	30 mL
Honey Dijon mustard	1 tbsp.	15 mL
Chopped fresh thyme leaves (or 1/2 tsp., 2 mL, dried)	1 1/2 tsp.	7 mL
Garlic clove, minced (or 1/4 tsp., 1 mL, powder)	1	1
Salt	1/4 tsp.	1 mL
Fresh spinach, stems removed, lightly packed	4 cups	1 L

Preheat electric grill for 5 minutes or gas barbecue to medium (to broil peppers and vegetables, see left). Arrange red pepper pieces, skin-side down, on greased grill. Cook for 10 to 15 minutes until skins are blistered and blackened. Transfer to small bowl. Cover with plastic wrap. Let sweat for about 15 minutes until cool enough to handle. Peel and discard skins. Cut into thin slices. Put into large bowl.

Cook zucchini slices on greased grill for about 5 minutes per side until grill marks appear. Cook yam slices on greased grill for 3 to 5 minutes per side until tender. Transfer to large plate. Cut zucchini and yam slices into bite-size pieces. Add to red pepper.

Balsamic Dressing: Combine first 6 ingredients in jar with tight-fitting lid. Shake well. Makes about 1/2 cup (125 mL) dressing. Drizzle over vegetables. Toss. Cover. Chill for 30 minutes to blend flavours.

Add spinach. Toss well. Serves 4.

1 serving: 174 Calories; 11 g Total Fat (7.6 g Mono, 1.2 g Poly, 1.5 g Sat); 0 mg Cholesterol; 18 g Carbohydrate; 5 g Fibre; 3 g Protein; 253 mg Sodium

Pictured on page 41.

Mixed Green Salad With Grilled Peppers

Red medium pepper, quartered	1	1
Yellow medium pepper, quartered	1	1
Croutons (recipe, right)		
Bags of mixed salad greens (4 1/2 oz., 128 g, each)	2	2
Can of romano beans, rinsed and drained	19 oz.	540 mL
Kalamata olives	1/2 cup	125 mL
Red medium onion, halved and thinly sliced	1	1
BASIL DRESSING		
Olive (or cooking) oil	1/3 cup	75 mL
Chopped fresh basil	3 tbsp.	50 mL
Red wine vinegar	2 tbsp.	30 mL
Garlic clove, minced (or 1/4 tsp., 1 mL, powder)	1	1
Granulated sugar	1 tsp.	5 mL
Salt	1/4 tsp.	1 mL
Pepper	1/8 tsp.	0.5 mL

Preheat electric grill for 5 minutes or gas barbecue to medium (to broil peppers, see page 42). Arrange red and yellow pepper pieces, skin-side down, on greased grill. Cook for 10 to 15 minutes until skins are blistered and blackened. Transfer to small bowl. Cover with plastic wrap. Let sweat for about 15 minutes until cool enough to handle. Peel and discard skins. Cut into 1/3 inch (1 cm) slices. Put into large bowl.

Add next 5 ingredients. Toss.

Basil Dressing: Process all 7 ingredients in blender or food processor until smooth. Makes about 1/2 cup (125 mL) dressing. Drizzle over salad. Toss gently. Serves 10 to 12.

1 serving: 166 Calories; 9.8 g Total Fat (6.7 g Mono, 1 g Poly, 1.6 g Sat); 0 mg Cholesterol; 17 g Carbohydrate; 3 g Fibre; 4 g Protein; 269 mg Sodium

Pictured on divider.

A variety of vibrant vegetables make this an eye-appealing salad.

croutons

Trim the crusts from 4 white bread slices. Cut the bread into small cubes. Melt 2 tbsp. (30 mL) hard margarine (or butter) in a large frying pan on medium. Add the bread cubes. Cook for 3 to 4 minutes, stirring occasionally, until golden. Remove the croutons to a paper towel-lined plate. Cool.

tip

To easily cut bread slices into cubes, partially freeze the bread first. Trim the crusts and cube a stack of 5 to 6 bread slices at once.

This salad makes a great lunch or light supper. It's also a nice first course before grilled fish, pork or chicken. For extra crunch, add some chopped celery or sliced water chestnuts.

Apple And Shrimp Salad

Head of romaine lettuce, chopped or torn	1	1
Bags of frozen cooked medium shrimp (12 oz., 340 g, each), peeled and deveined, thawed	2	2
Tart medium cooking apples (such as Granny Smith), with peel and thinly sliced	2	2
Chopped walnuts	1/2 cup	125 mL
Raisins	1/2 cup	125 mL
CREAMY DILL DRESSING		
Mayonnaise (or salad dressing)	1/4 cup	60 mL
Sour cream	1/4 cup	60 mL
Olive (or cooking) oil	3 tbsp.	50 mL
White wine vinegar	2 tbsp.	30 mL
Chopped fresh dill (or 1 1/2 tsp., 7 mL, dill weed)	2 tbsp.	30 mL
Granulated sugar	2 tsp.	10 mL
Salt	3/4 tsp.	4 mL
Pepper	1/4 tsp.	1 mL

Put first 5 ingredients into large bowl. Toss.

Creamy Dill Dressing: Process all 8 ingredients in blender or food processor until smooth. Makes about 3/4 cup (175 mL) dressing. Drizzle over salad. Toss well. Serves 8.

1 serving: 305 Calories; 17.9 g Total Fat (8.6 g Mono, 6 g Poly, 2.5 g Sat); 173 mg Cholesterol; 16 g Carbohydrate; 2 g Fibre; 21 g Protein; 460 mg Sodium

Pictured on page 41.

A colourful, delicately flavoured salad with soft bites of Brie, tangy cranberries and crunchy croutons. A delightful first course for any meal.

Cranberry Brie Salad

Dried cranberries	1/2 cup	125 mL
Port wine	1/4 cup	60 mL
Head of butter lettuce, chopped or torn	1	1
Croutons	2/3 cup	150 mL
Brie cheese round, chopped	4 oz.	113 g

(continued on next page)

CRANBERRY DRESSING

Cranberry cocktail	2 tbsp.	30 mL
Olive (or cooking) oil	2 tbsp.	30 mL
Basil pesto	1 tbsp.	15 mL
Red wine vinegar	1 tbsp.	15 mL

Measure cranberries and wine into small bowl. Stir until coated. Let stand for 1 hour, stirring occasionally. Drain. Transfer cranberries to large bowl.

Add lettuce, croutons and cheese. Toss.

Cranberry Dressing: Combine all 4 ingredients in jar with tight-fitting lid. Shake well. Makes about 1/3 cup (75 mL) dressing. Drizzle over salad. Toss well. Serves 4.

1 serving: 245 Calories; 17.3 g Total Fat (8.8 g Mono, 1.1 g Poly, 6.4 g Sat); 28 mg Cholesterol; 14 g Carbohydrate; 3 g Fibre; 8 g Protein; 269 mg Sodium

Pictured below.

about cranberries

The cranberry is indigenous to North America and grows wild in several provinces. Native peoples of North America used cranberries for food and medicine, but the Pilgrims, legend has it, popularized them, serving them at the first Thanksgiving. Today, British Columbia produces the majority of cranberries grown commercially in Canada, followed by Quebec, Nova Scotia, Ontario and New Brunswick.

A colourful, hearty salad with a zesty lemon kick. Sweet honey and a hint of garlic are nicely balanced.

about arugula

Arugula resembles radish leaves and has a distinct peppery flavour. Often included in commercial mixed salad greens, it can also be found in bags or in bunches with the roots still attached. For optimum freshness, place the roots in a glass of water, cover with a plastic bag, and store in the refrigerator for up to 2 days. Alternatively, wrap the roots with damp paper towels and put in a plastic bag before refrigerating. Discard the roots and stems and wash the leaves thoroughly before using.

Warm Chicken Salad

Chopped fresh rosemary leaves (or 1/2 tsp., 2 mL, dried, crushed)	2 tsp.	10 mL
Olive (or cooking) oil	1 tsp.	5 mL
Grated lemon zest	1 tsp.	5 mL
Garlic clove, minced (or 1/4 tsp., 1 mL, powder)	1	1
Pepper	1/2 tsp.	2 mL
Boneless, skinless chicken breast halves	1/2 lb.	225 g
Prosciutto (or deli ham) slices, cooked crisp and crumbled	8	8
Can of chickpeas (garbanzo beans), rinsed and drained	19 oz.	540 mL
Thinly sliced English cucumber (with peel)	3/4 cup	175 mL
Bag of arugula (or mixed salad greens)	4 1/2 oz.	128 g

LEMON GARLIC DRESSING		
Olive (or cooking) oil	1/3 cup	75 mL
Lemon juice	1/4 cup	60 mL
Liquid honey	2 tbsp.	30 mL
Garlic clove, minced (or 1/4 tsp., 1 mL, powder)	1	1
Hot pepper sauce	1/2 tsp.	2 mL
Salt	1/4 tsp.	1 mL
Pepper	1/4 tsp.	1 mL

Combine first 5 ingredients in medium bowl. Add chicken. Turn until coated. Cover. Chill for 30 minutes. Preheat electric grill for 5 minutes or gas barbecue to medium (see Note). Cook chicken on greased grill for about 5 minutes per side until no longer pink inside. Transfer to large plate. Cut into 1/4 inch (6 mm) slices. Put into large bowl.

Add next 4 ingredients. Toss.

(continued on next page)

Lemon Garlic Dressing: Combine all 7 ingredients in jar with tight-fitting lid. Shake well. Makes about 3/4 cup (175 mL) dressing. Drizzle over salad. Toss well. Serve immediately. Serves 6.

1 serving: 307 Calories; 19.4 g Total Fat (12.3 g Mono, 2.2 g Poly, 3.6 g Sat); 29 mg Cholesterol; 19 g Carbohydrate; 2 g Fibre; 15 g Protein; 346 mg Sodium

Pictured below.

Note: Chicken may be broiled in the oven instead of grilled. Place chicken on a greased broiler pan. Broil on the top rack for about 5 minutes per side until no longer pink inside.

A classic salad that often pops up at potlucks! A great way to get the kids to eat their broccoli.

broccoli slaw

Instead of broccoli florets, use 4 cups (1 L) broccoli slaw, available in bags in the produce section of your grocery store.

Broccoli Salad

Broccoli florets	5 cups	1.25 L
Bacon slices, cooked crisp and crumbled	6	6
Diced red onion	1/2 cup	125 mL
Grated medium Cheddar cheese	1/2 cup	125 mL
Salted, roasted sunflower seeds (optional)	1/4 cup	60 mL
SWEET CREAMY DRESSING		
Light salad dressing (or light mayonnaise)	6 tbsp.	100 mL
Granulated sugar	2 tbsp.	30 mL
White vinegar	2 tbsp.	30 mL

Put first 5 ingredients into large bowl. Toss.

Sweet Creamy Dressing: Combine salad dressing, sugar and vinegar in small bowl. Makes about 1/2 cup (125 mL) dressing. Drizzle over salad. Toss well. Serves 6.

1 serving: 164 Calories; 10.5 g Total Fat (4.7 g Mono, 1.7 g Poly, 3.5 g Sat); 16 mg Cholesterol; 12 g Carbohydrate; 2 g Fibre; 7 g Protein; 299 mg Sodium

Pictured on page 49.

A good addition to a luncheon served on the patio. Garnish with slices of red pepper for an extra splash of colour.

variation

For an equally delicious salad, use 1/4 cup (60 mL) thinly sliced red onion instead of the green onions.

Bacon And Pea Salad

Bacon slices, cooked crisp and crumbled	5	5
Cold cooked peas	3 cups	750 mL
Light sour cream	1/3 cup	75 mL
Green onions, sliced	4	4
Chopped fresh dill (or 1/4 tsp., 1 mL, dill weed)	1 tsp.	5 mL
Salt	1/2 tsp.	2 mL
Pepper, sprinkle		

Combine all 7 ingredients in medium bowl. Serves 4.

1 serving: 164 Calories; 5.7 g Total Fat (2.7 g Mono, 0.7 g Poly, 3.2 g Sat); 11 mg Cholesterol; 19 g Carbohydrate; 6 g Fibre; 10 g Protein; 543 mg Sodium

Pictured on page 49.

Clockwise from Top Right:
Bacon And Pea Salad, above
Cheesy Pea Salad, page 50
Broccoli Salad, above
Carrot Salad, page 50

A lovely salad to serve with grilled cheese sandwiches, hamburgers or hot dogs. Great for a picnic lunch, too!

Cheesy Pea Salad

Large hard-cooked eggs, chopped	3	3
Cold cooked peas	2 cups	500 mL
Thinly sliced celery	1 cup	250 mL
Diced light sharp Cheddar cheese	1/2 cup	125 mL
Sweet pickle relish	1/3 cup	75 mL
Salt, sprinkle		
Pepper, sprinkle		
CREAMY DRESSING		
Light salad dressing (or light mayonnaise)	1/4 cup	60 mL
Milk	1 1/2 tbsp.	25 mL
Granulated sugar	1/4 tsp.	1 mL

Combine first 7 ingredients in medium bowl.

Creamy Dressing: Combine salad dressing, milk and sugar in small bowl. Makes about 1/4 cup (60 mL) dressing. Drizzle over salad. Toss well. Serves 6.

1 serving: 177 Calories; 8.9 g Total Fat (3.6 g Mono, 1.3 g Poly, 3.1 g Sat); 118 mg Cholesterol; 16 g Carbohydrate; 3 g Fibre; 9 g Protein; 358 mg Sodium

Pictured on page 49.

Colourful carrot salad accented with sweet raisins. This is a delicious classic, enjoyed by many throughout the years.

cranberry carrot salad

Instead of raisins, use the same amount of dried cranberries for a tangy burst of flavour.

Carrot Salad

Grated carrot	3 cups	750 mL
Chopped celery	1/2 cup	125 mL
Raisins	1/2 cup	125 mL
CREAMY MUSTARD DRESSING		
Salad dressing (or mayonnaise)	1/2 cup	125 mL
White vinegar	1 tbsp.	15 mL
Granulated sugar	1 1/2 tsp.	7 mL
Prepared mustard	1/4 tsp.	1 mL
Paprika	1/8 tsp.	0.5 mL

(continued on next page)

Put carrot, celery and raisins into medium bowl. Toss.

Creamy Mustard Dressing: Combine all 5 ingredients in small bowl. Makes about 1/4 cup (60 mL) dressing. Drizzle over salad. Toss well. Serves 4.

1 serving: 258 Calories; 15.5 g Total Fat (8.4 g Mono, 5.2 g Poly, 1.2 g Sat); 8 mg Cholesterol; 30 g Carbohydrate; 3 g Fibre; 2 g Protein; 246 mg Sodium

Pictured on page 49.

Vegetable Marinade

Small head of cauliflower, separated into florets	1	1
Broccoli florets	3 cups	750 mL
Cherry tomatoes	2 cups	500 mL
Celery ribs, cut into 1 inch (2.5 cm) pieces	3	3
Medium carrots, cut into 1 inch (2.5 cm) pieces	3	3
Fresh whole white mushrooms (or two 10 oz., 284 mL, cans of whole mushrooms, drained)	2 cups	500 mL
Green medium pepper, cut into strips or rings	1	1
Italian dressing	1 cup	250 mL

Put first 7 ingredients into large bowl. Toss.

Drizzle dressing over vegetables. Toss until coated. Cover. Chill for at least 6 hours or overnight, tossing occasionally. Drain. Serves 12.

1 serving: 172 Calories; 14.7 g Total Fat (8 g Mono, 4.9 g Poly, 1.1 g Sat); 14 mg Cholesterol; 10 g Carbohydrate; 3 g Fibre; 3 g Protein; 377 mg Sodium

So simple to make and so delicious! Mix and match your favourite fresh vegetables according to your family's tastes. Toss veggies with our Italian Dressing, page 104, for an extra-fresh flavour.

variation

Instead of using Italian dressing, toss the vegetables with the same amount of Ginger Dressing or Sesame Soy Dressing, page 112, for a tasty change of pace.

A delicious salad that's always a hit. Makes lots, so it's a great potluck choice as well.

tip

To toast almonds and sesame seeds, spread them in a single layer in separate ungreased shallow pans. Bake in a 350°F (175°C) oven for 5 to 10 minutes, stirring or shaking often, until desired doneness.

japanese shrimp salad

Add 2 cups (500 mL) cooked small shrimp (peeled and deveined), and 1/2 cup (125 mL) each of sliced English cucumber (with peel) and sliced radish before tossing salad with dressing.

oriental chicken salad

Add 2 cups (500 mL) chopped cooked chicken, and 1/2 cup (125 mL) each of sliced English cucumber (with peel) and sliced radish before tossing salad with dressing.

Japanese Cabbage Salad

Medium head of cabbage, shredded	1/2	1/2
Fresh bean sprouts	4 1/2 cups	1.1 L
Sliced fresh white mushrooms	2 cups	500 mL
Sliced or slivered almonds, toasted (see Tip)	1/2 cup	125 mL
Raw sunflower seeds	1/4 cup	60 mL
Sesame seeds, toasted (see Tip)	2 tbsp.	30 mL
Green onions, chopped	2	2
ASIAN DRESSING		
Seasoning packet from instant noodles		
Cooking (or olive) oil	1/2 cup	125 mL
White vinegar	3 tbsp.	50 mL
Soy sauce	2 – 4 tbsp.	30 – 60 mL
Granulated sugar	1 tbsp.	15 mL
Salt	1 tsp.	5 mL
Pepper	1/2 tsp.	2 mL
Package of instant noodles with chicken-flavoured seasoning packet	3 oz.	85 g
Dry chow mein noodles	1 1/2 cups	375 mL

Put first 7 ingredients into large bowl. Toss.

Asian Dressing: Empty seasoning packet into jar with tight-fitting lid. Add next 6 ingredients. Shake well. Makes about 3/4 cup (175 mL) dressing. Drizzle over salad. Toss well.

Just before serving, break up instant noodles. Scatter over top. Sprinkle with chow mein noodles. Serves 10 to 12.

1 serving: 297 Calories; 23.2 g Total Fat (11.1 g Mono, 8.7 g Poly, 2.2 g Sat); 0 mg Cholesterol; 20 g Carbohydrate; 3 g Fibre; 6 g Protein; 593 mg Sodium

Pictured on page 53.

Serve this delicious side salad with barbecued ribs or pork chops. Store in the refrigerator for up to 2 days.

time saver

Make this coleslaw more quickly by using a package of coleslaw mix, available in the produce section of your grocery store.

Creamy Celery Seed Slaw

Shredded green cabbage, lightly packed	3 cups	750 mL
Shredded red cabbage, lightly packed	2 cups	500 mL
Grated carrot	3/4 cup	175 mL
Thinly sliced green onion	1/4 cup	60 mL
CELERY SEED DRESSING		
Mayonnaise (or salad dressing)	1 cup	250 mL
Apple cider vinegar	2 tbsp.	30 mL
Granulated sugar	2 tbsp.	30 mL
Chopped fresh parsley (or 3/4 tsp., 4 mL, flakes)	1 tbsp.	15 mL
Celery seed	1 1/2 tsp.	7 mL
Salt	1/4 tsp.	1 mL

Put first 4 ingredients into large bowl. Toss.

Celery Seed Dressing: Combine all 6 ingredients in small bowl. Makes about 1 1/4 cups (300 mL) dressing. Drizzle over cabbage mixture. Toss well. Chill for 1 hour to blend flavours. Serves 6.

1 serving: 326 Calories; 31.5 g Total Fat (17.4 g Mono, 10.5 g Poly, 3 g Sat); 23 mg Cholesterol; 11 g Carbohydrate; 2 g Fibre; 2 g Protein; 316 mg Sodium

Pictured on page 55.

A crisp, sweet slaw. Sure to become a favourite. Keeps in the refrigerator for up to a week.

Overnight Coleslaw

Medium head of cabbage, shredded	1	1
Medium onion, thinly sliced	1	1
Green medium pepper, cut into short thin strips	1	1
White vinegar	1 cup	250 mL
Cooking oil	2/3 cup	150 mL
Granulated sugar	1/2 cup	125 mL
Prepared mustard	2 tsp.	10 mL
Celery seed	1 tsp.	5 mL
Salt	1 tsp.	5 mL
Pepper	1/4 tsp.	1 mL

(continued on next page)

Put cabbage, onion and green pepper into large bowl. Toss.

Measure remaining 7 ingredients into medium saucepan. Heat on medium-high, stirring occasionally, until boiling. Boil for 1 minute. Drizzle over vegetables. Stir well. Press vegetables with spoon into vinegar mixture. Cover. Chill for at least 6 hours or overnight to blend flavours. Serves 10.

1 serving: 213 Calories; 15.8 g Total Fat (9.1 g Mono, 4.8 g Poly, 1.2 g Sat); 0 mg Cholesterol; 19 g Carbohydrate; 2 g Fibre; 2 g Protein; 271 mg Sodium

Pictured below.

Left: Creamy Celery Seed Slaw, page 54
Right: Overnight Coleslaw, page 54

A unique salad combination. Increase the amount of chili paste if you'd like a little more heat.

tip

To toast cashews, spread them in a single layer in an ungreased shallow pan. Bake in a 350°F (175°C) oven for 5 to 10 minutes, stirring or shaking often, until desired doneness.

about blanching

Salad recipes call for blanching to brighten the colour of fresh vegetables and help maintain their crispness. To blanch vegetables, immerse small batches briefly in boiling water (photo 1), then immediately plunge them into ice water to stop the cooking process. Leave vegetables in the water until cold, changing the water if it warms (photo 2).

Blanching times vary, from 30 seconds to 5 or more minutes, depending on the vegetable. Start timing once the water is boiling again. Be sure to follow your recipe carefully so that vegetables are blanched, and not cooked through.

Bean And Cashew Salad

Fresh whole green beans	1/2 lb.	225 g
Boiling water		
Ice water		
Halved cherry tomatoes	2 cups	500 mL
Plain cashews, toasted (see Tip)	1 cup	250 mL
Thinly sliced red onion	3/4 cup	175 mL
LEMON DILL DRESSING		
Olive (or cooking) oil	1/3 cup	75 mL
Lemon juice	3 tbsp.	50 mL
Chopped fresh dill (or 1/2 tsp., 2 mL, dill weed)	2 tsp.	10 mL
Garlic clove, minced (or 1/4 tsp., 1 mL, powder)	1	1
Chili paste (sambal oelek)	1/2 tsp.	2 mL
Salt	1/4 tsp.	1 mL

Blanch beans in boiling water in large saucepan for 1 to 3 minutes until bright green. Drain. Immediately plunge into ice water in large bowl. Let stand for about 10 minutes until cold. Drain. Transfer to separate large bowl.

Add tomato, cashews and onion. Toss.

Lemon Dill Dressing: Combine all 6 ingredients in jar with tight-fitting lid. Shake well. Makes about 1/2 cup (125 mL) dressing. Drizzle over salad. Toss well. Serves 8.

1 serving: 211 Calories; 18 g Total Fat (11.9 g Mono, 2.3 g Poly, 3 g Sat); 0 mg Cholesterol; 11 g Carbohydrate; 1 g Fibre; 4 g Protein; 82 mg Sodium

Pictured on page 57.

Use a slotted spoon to serve this colourful, tasty salad. Double the onion rings if you like more. Makes lots—a real crowd pleaser!

tip

Rinsing and draining canned beans removes much of the sodium used in the canning process. It also enhances their appearance for use in salads by removing the canning liquid. In marinated salads, the liquid from canned beans may be used to contribute extra flavour to the marinade.

Bean Salad

Can of cut green beans (do not drain)	14 oz.	398 mL
Can of cut yellow wax beans, rinsed and drained	14 oz.	398 mL
Can of lima beans, rinsed and drained	14 oz.	398 mL
Can of kidney beans, rinsed and drained	14 oz.	398 mL
Small onion, sliced and separated into rings	1	1
Sliced celery	1 cup	250 mL
Jar of pimiento, well drained and chopped	2 oz.	57 mL
Granulated sugar	1 cup	250 mL
Dry mustard	1/2 tsp.	2 mL
Salt	1/4 tsp.	1 mL
White vinegar	1 cup	250 mL
Cooking oil	2 tbsp.	30 mL

Put green beans with liquid into large bowl. Add next 6 ingredients. Stir.

Combine sugar, mustard and salt in small bowl. Add vinegar and cooking oil. Stir until sugar is dissolved. Drizzle over salad. Stir. Cover. Chill for 24 hours to blend flavours. Store in refrigerator for up to 3 weeks. Serves 16.

1 serving: 72 Calories; 1.2 g Total Fat (0.7 g Mono, 0.4 g Poly, 0.1 g Sat); 0 mg Cholesterol; 14 g Carbohydrate; 1 g Fibre; 2 g Protein; 107 mg Sodium

Pictured on page 59.

An easy salad. Cool and refreshing.

variation

For a sweet, tangy dressing, add 2 tbsp. (30 mL) each of lemon juice, chopped fresh parsley and granulated sugar to the sour cream mixture.

Cucumbers In Sour Cream

English cucumbers (with peel)	3	3
Salt	1 1/2 tsp.	7 mL
Sour cream	1 cup	250 mL
Chopped fresh dill (or 1/2 tsp., 2 mL, dill weed)	2 tsp.	10 mL

Score cucumbers (see Note). Thinly slice. Put into large bowl. Sprinkle with salt. Stir. Cover. Chill for 1 hour. Drain.

(continued on next page)

Combine sour cream and dill in small bowl. Add to cucumber. Stir until coated.
Serves 12.

1 serving: 42 Calories; 3 g Total Fat (0.8 g Mono, 0.2 g Poly, 1.8 g Sat); 8 mg Cholesterol; 3 g Carbohydrate;
1 g Fibre; 1 g Protein; 159 mg Sodium

Pictured below.

Note: To score a cucumber, drag a fork or a zesting tool lengthwise down the
peel, using an even pressure. Repeat all around the cucumber to create a pretty
green and white striped effect.

Left: Cucumbers In Sour Cream, page 58
Right: Bean Salad, page 58

You won't be able to stop eating these once you start! They have a great sweet and sour flavour.

Crispy Cukes

White vinegar	1 cup	250 mL
Granulated sugar	1 cup	250 mL
Water	1 cup	250 mL
Salt	1 tbsp.	15 mL
Pepper	1/4 tsp.	1 mL
Onion powder	1/4 tsp.	1 mL
English cucumbers (with peel)	4	4

Measure first 6 ingredients into large bowl. Stir until sugar is dissolved.

Score cucumbers (see Note). Cut into thin slices. Add to vinegar mixture. Stir. Cover. Chill for 24 hours to blend flavours. Store in refrigerator for up to 1 week. Serves 8.

1 serving: 129 Calories; 0.2 g Total Fat (0 g Mono, 0.1 g Poly, 0.1 g Sat); 0 mg Cholesterol; 33 g Carbohydrate; 1 g Fibre; 1 g Protein; 888 mg Sodium

Pictured on page 63.

Note: To score a cucumber, drag a fork or a zesting tool lengthwise down the peel, using an even pressure. Repeat all around the cucumber to create a pretty green and white striped effect.

Chickpeas pack this delicious, crunchy salad with protein. A great choice for lunch! This salad may be stored in the refrigerator for up to 3 days.

Chickpea Tomato Salad

Can of chickpeas (garbanzo beans), rinsed and drained	19 oz.	540 mL
Can of stewed tomatoes, drained and chopped	14 oz.	398 mL
Thinly sliced celery	1/2 cup	125 mL
Diced red pepper	1/2 cup	125 mL
Green onion, thinly sliced	1	1

(continued on next page)

BASIL MUSTARD DRESSING

Olive (or cooking) oil	2 tbsp.	30 mL
White vinegar	2 tbsp.	30 mL
Chopped fresh parsley (or 2 tsp., 10 mL, flakes)	2 1/2 tbsp.	37 mL
Chopped fresh basil (or 1/2 tsp., 2 mL, dried)	2 tsp.	10 mL
Dry mustard	1/4 tsp.	1 mL
Garlic powder	1/8 tsp.	0.5 mL

tip

For easier preparation, make marinated salads in bowls or other containers with tight-fitting lids. Turn the container over occasionally, instead of stirring the salad, to distribute the marinade evenly.

Put first 5 ingredients into medium bowl. Stir.

Basil Mustard Dressing: Combine all 6 ingredients in small bowl. Makes about 1/4 cup (60 mL) dressing. Drizzle over salad. Stir. Cover. Chill for at least 6 hours or overnight, stirring occasionally. Serves 6.

1 serving: 131 Calories; 5.8 g Total Fat (3.6 g Mono, 0.9 g Poly, 0.8 g Sat); 0 mg Cholesterol; 17 g Carbohydrate; 3 g Fibre; 4 g Protein; 288 mg Sodium

Pictured below.

A wonderful combination of fresh tastes in a colourful, summery salad.

Tomato Pineapple Salad

Roma (plum) tomatoes, quartered lengthwise	6	6
Can of pineapple tidbits, drained	14 oz.	398 mL
Thinly sliced red onion	1/4 cup	60 mL
Coarsely chopped fresh basil (or 1 1/2 tsp., 7 mL, dried)	2 tbsp.	30 mL
CHILI GARLIC DRESSING		
Cooking oil	2 tbsp.	30 mL
White (or red) wine vinegar	2 tbsp.	30 mL
Garlic clove, minced (or 1/4 tsp., 1 mL, powder)	1	1
Dried crushed chilies	1/4 tsp.	1 mL
Salt	1/4 tsp.	1 mL
Pepper	1/4 tsp.	1 mL
Coarsely chopped pecans, toasted (see Tip)	1/3 cup	75 mL

Put first 4 ingredients into medium bowl. Toss gently.

Chili Garlic Dressing: Combine first 6 ingredients in jar with tight-fitting lid. Shake well. Makes about 1/4 cup (60 mL) dressing. Drizzle over salad. Toss gently.

Sprinkle with pecans. Serves 6.

1 serving: 139 Calories; 9.8 g Total Fat (5.7 g Mono, 2.7 g Poly, 0.8 g Sat); 0 mg Cholesterol; 14 g Carbohydrate; 3 g Fibre; 2 g Protein; 112 mg Sodium

Pictured on page 63.

Clockwise from Top Right:
Creamy Corn Salad, page 64
Tomato Pineapple Salad, above
Beet Salad, page 66
Crispy Cukes, page 60

A salad you just have to try! Deliciously spiced and bursting with colour.

storing garlic

Fresh garlic should be stored at room temperature in a cool, dry place. Refrigeration will dehydrate the cloves, affecting the garlic's flavour, and may result in other refrigerated foods absorbing its odour.

Creamy Corn Salad

Can of black beans, rinsed and drained	14 oz.	398 mL
Can of kernel corn, drained	12 oz.	341 mL
Medium tomatoes, seeds removed, finely chopped	2	2
Finely chopped red onion	1/2 cup	125 mL
Finely chopped red pepper	1/2 cup	125 mL
Chopped fresh cilantro or parsley (optional)	2 tbsp.	30 mL

SPICY RANCH DRESSING		
Ranch dressing	1/4 cup	60 mL
Lime juice	1 tbsp.	15 mL
Ground cumin	1/4 tsp.	1 mL
Chili powder	1/4 tsp.	1 mL
Garlic clove, minced (or 1/4 tsp., 1 mL, powder)	1	1
Salt	1/4 tsp.	1 mL

Put first 6 ingredients into large bowl. Toss.

Spicy Ranch Dressing: Combine all 6 ingredients in small bowl. Makes about 2/3 cup (150 mL) dressing. Drizzle over salad. Toss well. Serves 6.

1 serving: 150 Calories; 4.6 g Total Fat (2.3 g Mono, 1.6 g Poly, 0.4 g Sat); 3 mg Cholesterol; 24 g Carbohydrate; 4 g Fibre; 5 g Protein; 395 mg Sodium

Pictured on page 63.

This unique combination of nippy radishes, sweet oranges and spices is certain to enliven dinner.

Radish And Orange Salad

Thinly sliced radish	3 cups	750 mL
Can of mandarin orange segments, drained	10 oz.	284 mL
Slivered almonds, toasted (see Tip)	1/3 cup	75 mL
Sliced green onion	1/4 cup	60 mL
Dried crushed chilies	3/4 – 1 tsp.	4 – 5 mL

(continued on next page)

CHILI BASIL DRESSING

Olive (or cooking) oil	3 tbsp.	50 mL
White wine vinegar	2 tbsp.	30 mL
Chopped fresh basil (or 3/4 tsp., 4 mL, dried)	1 tbsp.	15 mL
Chili powder	1/4 tsp.	1 mL
Ground coriander	1/8 tsp.	0.5 mL
Salt	1/8 tsp.	0.5 mL
Pepper	1/8 tsp.	0.5 mL

tip

To toast almonds, spread them in a single layer in an ungreased shallow pan. Bake in a 350°F (175°C) oven for 5 to 10 minutes, stirring or shaking often, until desired doneness.

Put first 5 ingredients into medium bowl. Toss gently.

Chili Basil Dressing: Combine all 7 ingredients in jar with tight-fitting lid. Shake well. Makes about 1/3 cup (75 mL) dressing. Drizzle over salad. Toss gently. Serves 4.

1 serving: 198 Calories; 16.9 g Total Fat (11.5 g Mono, 2.2 g Poly, 2 g Sat); 0 mg Cholesterol; 12 g Carbohydrate; 3 g Fibre; 3 g Protein; 109 mg Sodium

Pictured below.

Brightly coloured and crunchy good! A savoury twist on a Waldorf salad.

Beet Salad

Cans of sliced beets (14 oz., 398 mL, each), drained and diced	2	2
Sliced celery	1 cup	250 mL
Medium apple, peeled and diced	1	1
Chopped walnuts	1/4 cup	60 mL
Salt	1/2 tsp.	2 mL
CREAMY HORSERADISH DRESSING		
Sour cream	1/4 cup	60 mL
Mayonnaise (or salad dressing)	1/4 cup	60 mL
Prepared horseradish	1/2 tsp.	2 mL

Combine first 5 ingredients in large bowl.

Creamy Horseradish Dressing: Combine sour cream, mayonnaise and horseradish in small bowl. Makes about 1/2 cup (125 mL) dressing. Drizzle over salad. Toss gently. Serves 8.

1 serving: 119 Calories; 9.5 g Total Fat (4.1 g Mono, 3.6 g Poly, 1.4 g Sat); 7 mg Cholesterol; 8 g Carbohydrate; 2 g Fibre; 2 g Protein; 351 mg Sodium

Pictured on page 63.

This not-so-common salad is excellent. Try it for a change from the ordinary.

Bean Sprout Salad

Snow peas, trimmed	6 oz.	170 g
Boiling water		
Ice water		
Fresh bean sprouts	4 1/2 cups	1.1 L
Shredded cabbage, lightly packed	1 cup	250 mL
Chopped pimiento	2 tbsp.	30 mL
SOY DRESSING		
Cooking oil	2 tbsp.	30 mL
Soy sauce	2 tbsp.	30 mL
White vinegar	2 tbsp.	30 mL
Brown sugar, packed	2 tbsp.	30 mL

(continued on next page)

Blanch snow peas in boiling water in medium saucepan for about 1 minute until bright green. Drain. Immediately plunge into ice water in large bowl. Let stand for about 10 minutes until cold. Drain. Transfer to separate large bowl.

Add bean sprouts, cabbage and pimiento. Toss.

Soy Dressing: Combine all 4 ingredients in small bowl. Makes about 1/3 cup (75 mL) dressing. Drizzle over salad. Toss well. Serves 6.

1 serving: 97 Calories; 4.9 g Total Fat (2.7 g Mono, 1.5 g Poly, 0.4 g Sat); 0 mg Cholesterol; 12 g Carbohydrate; 2 g Fibre; 4 g Protein; 358 mg Sodium

Pictured below.

Three fruits mingle in a tasty jellied salad. Excellent with roast turkey or chicken.

tip

To successfully unmold a gelatin salad, first make sure it is completely set. Gently loosen the gelatin from the edge of the mold or pan using damp fingers or a spatula dipped in warm water. Dip the mold into warm (not hot) water for about 15 seconds. Place a serving plate on top of the mold and invert both the mold and plate. Shake slightly to loosen. Carefully remove the mold. If the gelatin does not release easily, dip the mold into warm water again for a few seconds.

Cranberry Jelly Salad

Box of cherry-flavoured jelly powder (gelatin)	3 oz.	85 g
Envelope of unflavoured gelatin (about 1 tbsp., 15 mL)	1/4 oz.	7 g
Boiling water	1 1/4 cups	300 mL
Can of crushed pineapple (with juice)	14 oz.	398 mL
Can of whole cranberry sauce	14 oz.	398 mL
Finely diced red apple (with peel)	1/2 cup	125 mL

Combine jelly powder and gelatin in medium bowl. Add boiling water. Stir until dissolved.

Add pineapple with juice, cranberry sauce and apple. Stir. Chill, stirring occasionally, until slightly thickened. Pour into lightly greased 4 1/2 to 5 cup (1.1 to 1.25 L) mold. Chill for 2 to 3 hours until set. Serves 8.

1 serving: 167 Calories; 0.2 g Total Fat (0 g Mono, 0 g Poly, 0 g Sat); 0 mg Cholesterol; 42 g Carbohydrate; 1 g Fibre; 2 g Protein; 46 mg Sodium

Pictured on page 69.

Clockwise from Top Left:
Apricot Salad, page 70
Apricot Sauce, page 70
Cranberry Jelly Salad, above
Cherry Cheese Salad, page 71

A beautiful salad and a heavenly sauce! Garnish with canned apricot halves for a fabulous finishing touch.

pretty presentation

Instead of using a mold, pour the salad mixture into a lightly greased 9 x 9 inch (22 x 22 cm) pan. Chill until set. Cut into squares and spoon the sauce over individual servings.

Apricot Salad

Boxes of orange-flavoured jelly powder (gelatin), 3 oz. (85 g), each	2	2
Boiling water	1 1/2 cups	375 mL
Jars of strained apricot baby food (4 1/2 oz., 128 mL, each)	2	2
Can of crushed pineapple (with juice)	14 oz.	398 mL
APRICOT SAUCE		
Granulated sugar	1/2 cup	125 mL
All-purpose flour	3 tbsp.	50 mL
Jar of strained apricot baby food	4 1/2 oz.	128 mL
Pineapple juice	1/2 cup	125 mL
Whipping cream (see Note)	1 cup	250 mL
Grated medium Cheddar cheese	1 cup	250 mL

Empty jelly powder into large bowl. Add boiling water. Stir until dissolved.

Add strained apricot and pineapple with juice. Stir. Chill, stirring often, until starting to thicken. Pour into lightly greased 4 1/2 cup (1.1 L) mold. Chill until set.

Apricot Sauce: Combine sugar and flour in small saucepan.

Add strained apricot and pineapple juice. Heat and stir on medium for about 5 minutes until boiling and thickened. Cool. Transfer to medium bowl. Chill.

Beat whipping cream in small bowl until stiff peaks form. Fold about 1/3 of whipped cream into apricot mixture to lighten. Fold in remaining whipped cream and cheese. Makes about 3 cups (750 mL) sauce. Serve with salad. Serves 8.

1 serving: 453 Calories; 15.2 g Total Fat (4.4 g Mono, 0.5 g Poly, 9.5 g Sat); 52 mg Cholesterol; 77 g Carbohydrate; 1 g Fibre; 7 g Protein; 181 mg Sodium

Pictured on page 69.

Note: If preferred, use 1 envelope of dessert topping (prepared) instead of the whipping cream. This salad will be a bit sweeter, but still very good.

Cherry Cheese Salad

Box of raspberry-flavoured jelly powder (gelatin)	3 oz.	85 g
Boiling water	1 cup	250 mL
Can of cherry pie filling	19 oz.	540 mL
Box of lemon-flavoured jelly powder (gelatin)	3 oz.	85 g
Boiling water	1 cup	250 mL
Block of cream cheese, softened	4 oz.	125 g
Salad dressing (or mayonnaise)	1/3 cup	75 mL
Crushed pineapple (with juice)	1 cup	250 mL
Whipping cream (see Note)	1 cup	250 mL
Miniature marshmallows	1 1/2 cups	375 mL
Chopped walnuts	2 tbsp.	30 mL
Green leaf lettuce leaves	9	9

This colourful, creamy salad is just right for a bridal shower or a club get-together.

another pretty presentation

Instead of cutting into individual pieces, invert the entire salad onto a lettuce-lined serving platter. To loosen, place a warm, damp tea towel on the bottom of the pan. Gently shake the pan and platter until the salad releases. Beautiful for a buffet!

Empty raspberry jelly powder into large bowl. Add first amount of boiling water. Stir until dissolved. Add pie filling. Stir. Spread evenly in lightly greased 9 x 9 inch (22 x 22 cm) pan. Chill until almost set.

Empty lemon jelly powder into small bowl. Add second amount of boiling water. Stir until dissolved.

Beat cream cheese and salad dressing in separate large bowl until smooth. Add lemon jelly powder mixture and pineapple with juice. Stir well. Chill until slightly thickened.

Beat whipping cream in medium bowl until stiff peaks form. Fold into cream cheese mixture. Fold in marshmallows. Spread on top of cherry layer in pan.

Sprinkle with walnuts. Chill until set. Cut into 9 pieces. Serve on lettuce leaves on individual salad plates. Serves 9.

1 serving: 382 Calories; 19.5 g Total Fat (6.8 g Mono, 2.7 g Poly, 9.1 g Sat); 50 mg Cholesterol; 51 g Carbohydrate; 1 g Fibre; 4 g Protein; 167 mg Sodium

Pictured on page 69.

Note: If preferred, use 1 envelope of dessert topping (prepared) instead of the whipping cream. This salad will be a bit sweeter, but still very good.

This refreshing salad goes well with just about anything.

perfect cucumber salad

Omit the sour cream. Pour the entire amount of slightly thickened cucumber mixture into the mold. Chill until set. Makes a sparkling clear salad.

cucumber sour cream salad

Increase the sour cream to 1 cup (250 mL). Add to the entire amount of slightly thickened cucumber mixture. Stir. Pour into the mold. Chill until set. Makes a completely different salad—creamy and soft.

A tropical delight! The presentation of this refreshing, healthy fruit salad is perfect for a buffet luncheon.

Layered Cucumber Salad

Box of lime-flavoured jelly powder (gelatin)	3 oz.	85 g
Boiling water	1/2 cup	125 mL
Finely grated English cucumber (with peel)	1 cup	250 mL
Finely chopped onion (or 1 tbsp., 15 mL, onion flakes)	1/4 cup	60 mL
Lemon juice	2 tbsp.	30 mL
Salt	1/4 tsp.	1 mL
Sour cream	1/2 cup	125 mL

Empty jelly powder into large bowl. Add boiling water. Stir until dissolved.

Add next 4 ingredients. Stir. Chill, stirring occasionally, until slightly thickened. Spoon 1/2 of cucumber mixture into lightly greased 3 cup (750 mL) mold. Chill until almost set. Chill remaining cucumber mixture in bowl until almost set.

Add sour cream to cucumber mixture in bowl. Stir. Spread over layer in mold. Chill until set. Serves 6.

1 serving: 91 Calories; 2.9 g Total Fat (0.8 g Mono, 0.1 g Poly, 1.8 g Sat); 8 mg Cholesterol; 15 g Carbohydrate; trace Fibre; 2 g Protein; 144 mg Sodium

Pineapple Boat Salad

Fresh pineapple (with leaves attached), halved lengthwise	1	1
Halved fresh strawberries	1 cup	250 mL
Halved seedless green (or red) grapes	1/2 cup	125 mL
Kiwifruit, sliced	1	1
Medium banana, sliced	1	1
1% cottage cheese	1 cup	250 mL
Chopped pecans (or walnuts)	1/4 cup	60 mL
Chopped green onion	1 tbsp.	15 mL
Chopped pecans (or walnuts), for garnish		

(continued on next page)

Remove and discard core from each pineapple half. Cut out pineapple, leaving 1/2 inch (12 mm) shell. Cut pineapple into bite-size pieces. Put into medium bowl.

Add next 4 ingredients. Toss gently. Spoon into each pineapple half.

Combine cottage cheese, first amount of pecans and green onion. Spoon on top of fruit mixture.

Garnish with second amount of pecans. Serves 4.

1 serving: *221 Calories; 6.9 g Total Fat (3.6 g Mono, 1.6 g Poly, 0.9 g Sat); 3 mg Cholesterol; 34 g Carbohydrate; 4 g Fibre; 10 g Protein; 253 mg Sodium*

Pictured below.

One, two, three and you're done! A not-too-sweet salad that will leave them wanting more.

Quick Fruit Salad

Miniature marshmallows	2 1/2 cups	625 mL
Can of fruit cocktail, drained	14 oz.	398 mL
Sour cream	1 cup	250 mL
Chopped walnuts	1/4 cup	60 mL
Lettuce leaves	4	4
Maraschino cherries	4	4

Combine first 4 ingredients in large bowl. Chill for at least 1 hour.

Arrange lettuce leaves on 4 salad plates. Spoon fruit cocktail mixture on top of each.

Top each with 1 cherry. Serves 4.

1 serving: 273 Calories; 13.4 g Total Fat (3.5 g Mono, 3.5 g Poly, 5.6 g Sat); 24 mg Cholesterol; 37 g Carbohydrate; 1 g Fibre; 5 g Protein; 45 mg Sodium

Pictured on page 77.

An old familiar favourite. Just as good as it's always been!

Old-Fashioned Waldorf

Diced peeled apple	1 cup	250 mL
Chopped celery	1 cup	250 mL
Halved seedless red grapes	1/2 cup	125 mL
Chopped walnuts	1/2 cup	125 mL
Whipping cream (see Note)	1 cup	250 mL
Granulated sugar	1/4 cup	60 mL
White vinegar	3 tbsp.	50 mL

Combine first 4 ingredients in medium bowl.

Beat whipping cream in small bowl until soft peaks form. Add sugar. Beat just until stiff peaks form. Add vinegar. Stir. Add to apple mixture. Fold gently. Serves 4.

1 serving: 380 Calories; 29.8 g Total Fat (8 g Mono, 6.9 g Poly, 13.3 g Sat); 73 mg Cholesterol; 27 g Carbohydrate; 2 g Fibre; 6 g Protein; 51 mg Sodium

Note: For equally good results, omit the whipping cream and granulated sugar and use 1 envelope of dessert topping, prepared.

Pistachio Salad

Box of instant pistachio pudding powder (4 serving size)	1	1
Milk	1 3/4 cups	425 mL
Miniature marshmallows	2 cups	500 mL
Can of crushed pineapple, drained	14 oz.	398 mL
Chopped walnuts (optional)	1/2 cup	125 mL
Whipping cream (see Note)	1 cup	250 mL
Lettuce leaves (or shredded lettuce)	8 – 10	8 – 10

Empty pudding powder into medium bowl. Add milk. Stir until smooth.

Add marshmallows, pineapple and walnuts. Stir.

Beat whipping cream in small bowl until stiff peaks form. Fold into pudding mixture. Chill. Serve on lettuce leaves on individual salad plates. Serves 8 to 10.

1 serving: 224 Calories; 10.9 g Total Fat (3.2 g Mono, 0.4 g Poly, 6.7 g Sat); 39 mg Cholesterol; 30 g Carbohydrate; trace Fibre; 3 g Protein; 231 mg Sodium

Note: If preferred, use 1 envelope of dessert topping (prepared) instead of the whipping cream. This salad will be a bit sweeter, but still very good.

Such a treat to eat, and so different. Good right out of the bowl or spooned over fresh fruit.

variation

For a more solid, less creamy salad, omit the milk and use the same amount of pineapple juice.

Rum and coconut add a tropical flair to this attractive salad. For those with a sweet tooth, more sugar may be added.

tip

To toast coconut, spread in a single layer in an ungreased shallow pan. Bake in a 350°F (175°C) oven for 5 to 10 minutes, stirring or shaking often, until desired doneness.

Rum Fruit Salad

Lime juice	1/3 cup	75 mL
Granulated sugar	1/3 cup	75 mL
Dark (navy) rum	1/4 cup	60 mL
Cubed papaya	2 cups	500 mL
Cubed fresh pineapple (or two 14 oz., 398 mL, cans of pineapple tidbits, drained)	2 cups	500 mL
Large oranges, peeled and segmented	4	4
Flake coconut, toasted (see Tip)	3 tbsp.	50 mL

Combine lime juice and sugar in small saucepan. Heat and stir on low for about 5 minutes until sugar is dissolved. Bring to a boil on medium-high. Boil gently, uncovered, for 3 to 5 minutes, stirring occasionally, until slightly thickened.

Add rum. Stir. Cool.

Put papaya, pineapple and orange segments into large bowl. Drizzle with rum mixture. Stir until coated. Chill for 3 hours, stirring occasionally.

Sprinkle with coconut. Serves 6.

1 serving: 186 Calories; 2.3 g Total Fat (0.2 g Mono, 0.2 g Poly, 1.7 g Sat); 0 mg Cholesterol; 38 g Carbohydrate; 4 g Fibre; 2 g Protein; 3 mg Sodium

Pictured on page 77.

Clockwise from Top Left:
Rum Fruit Salad, above
Apricot Dressing, page 78
Fresh Fruit Salad, page 78
Quick Fruit Salad, page 74

A festive presentation for a fruit salad! Any seasonal fruit will do. Experiment and use your imagination to arrange the fruit on the platter any way you like. Have fun!

Fresh Fruit Salad

APRICOT DRESSING

Dried apricots	8	8
Boiling water		
Vanilla yogurt	3/4 cup	175 mL
Fresh strawberries, halved	6	6
Kiwifruit, each cut lengthwise into 6 wedges	4	4
Seedless red grapes, halved	18	18
Cantaloupe balls or cubes	24	24
Fresh blueberries	1/2 cup	125 mL
Thin red apple wedges (with peel), dipped in lemon juice	12	12

Apricot Dressing: Put apricots into small bowl. Cover with boiling water. Let stand for about 20 minutes until softened. Drain. Transfer to blender or food processor. Add yogurt. Process until smooth. Makes about 3/4 cup (175 mL) dressing.

Arrange strawberries in centre of large serving platter. Arrange next 4 fruits in circular pattern around strawberries (see photo, page 77).

Place apple wedges, peel-side up, between fruit on platter. Drizzle dressing over salad or serve as dip on the side. Serves 6.

1 serving: 344 Calories; 1.7 g Total Fat (0.4 g Mono, 0.2 g Poly, 0.5 g Sat); 2 mg Cholesterol; 85 g Carbohydrate; 11 g Fibre; 6 g Protein; 40 mg Sodium

Pictured on page 77.

A healthy salad that's perfect for breakfast, brunch or lunch.

Summer Fruit Salad

Medium bananas, sliced	2	2
Honeydew balls	1 cup	250 mL
Fresh raspberries	1 cup	250 mL
Fresh blueberries	1 cup	250 mL
Fresh peach slices	1/2 cup	125 mL
Halved fresh strawberries	1/2 cup	125 mL

(continued on next page)

| 2% cottage cheese | 3 cups | 750 mL |
| Bread slices, toasted and halved diagonally (buttered, optional) | 6 | 6 |

SUMMER FRUIT TOPPING

| Frozen whipped topping, thawed | 1 cup | 250 mL |
| Light salad dressing (or light mayonnaise) | 4 tsp. | 20 mL |

Combine first 6 ingredients in large bowl.

Spoon cottage cheese onto centre of 6 salad plates. Spoon fruit mixture halfway around cottage cheese. Place 2 toast halves on opposite side of cottage cheese on each plate.

Summer Fruit Topping: Fold whipped topping into salad dressing in small bowl. Makes about 1 cup (250 mL) topping. Spoon over fruit. Serves 6.

1 serving: 307 Calories; 7.9 g Total Fat (1.8 g Mono, 0.7 g Poly, 4.7 g Sat); 10 mg Cholesterol; 41 g Carbohydrate; 4 g Fibre; 20 g Protein; 653 mg Sodium

Pictured below.

Full of colour and flavour, this pasta salad will dress up your meal or add pizzazz to your picnic.

about pesto

Classic Italian pesto is a rich, uncooked sauce made of crushed fresh basil, garlic, pine nuts, Parmesan cheese and olive oil. Pesto, including a sun-dried tomato variation, is available in most grocery stores.

Pesto Pasta Salad

Fusilli (or other spiral) pasta (about 1 lb., 454 g)	4 cups	1 L
Boiling water	16 cups	4 L
Salt	2 tsp.	10 mL
Cooked broccoli florets, chilled (see Note)	2 cups	500 mL
Cooked cauliflower florets, chilled	2 cups	500 mL
Cooked trimmed snow peas, chilled	2 cups	500 mL
Cooked sliced carrot, chilled	1 1/2 cups	375 mL
Sliced fresh white mushrooms	1 cup	250 mL
PESTO DRESSING		
Basil pesto	3/4 cup	175 mL
Olive (or cooking) oil	2/3 cup	150 mL
Grated Parmesan cheese	1/2 cup	125 mL
White vinegar	1/3 cup	75 mL
Salt	1 tsp.	5 mL

Cook pasta in boiling water and salt in large uncovered pot or Dutch oven for 8 to 10 minutes, stirring occasionally, until tender but firm. Drain. Rinse with cold water. Drain well. Transfer to large bowl.

Add next 5 ingredients. Toss.

Pesto Dressing: Combine all 5 ingredients in small bowl. Makes about 2 cups (500 mL) dressing. Drizzle over salad. Toss gently. Serves 8.

1 serving: 498 Calories; 26.2 g Total Fat (17.5 g Mono, 2.6 g Poly, 4.6 g Sat); 5 mg Cholesterol; 53 g Carbohydrate; 5 g Fibre; 14 g Protein; 462 mg Sodium

Pictured on page 81.

Note: Cook all vegetables just until tender-crisp for best results.

An inviting salad with a hearty helping of tasty ingredients. This Greek and Italian blend is sure to impress!

tip

To toast pine nuts, spread them in a single layer in an ungreased shallow pan. Bake in a 350°F (175°C) oven for 5 to 10 minutes, stirring or shaking often, until desired doneness.

Spinach Pasta Salad

Lemon juice	2 tbsp.	30 mL
Olive (or cooking) oil	1 tbsp.	15 mL
Garlic clove, minced (or 1/4 tsp., 1 mL, powder)	1	1
Boneless, skinless chicken breast halves	1/2 lb.	225 g
Medium bow (or other) pasta (about 6 oz., 170 g)	2 cups	500 mL
Boiling water	8 cups	2 L
Salt	1 tsp.	5 mL
Fresh spinach, stems removed, lightly packed	4 cups	1 L
Chopped tomato	1 cup	250 mL
Crumbled feta cheese (about 2 1/2 oz., 70 g)	1/2 cup	125 mL
Kalamata olives	1/3 cup	75 mL
PARSLEY PESTO DRESSING		
Coarsely chopped fresh parsley	1/2 cup	125 mL
Grated Parmesan cheese	1/3 cup	75 mL
Olive (or cooking) oil	1/3 cup	75 mL
Pine nuts, toasted (see Tip)	1/4 cup	60 mL
Red wine vinegar	1/4 cup	60 mL
Garlic cloves, minced (or 1/2 tsp., 2 mL, powder)	2	2
Salt	1/4 tsp.	1 mL
Pepper	1/8 tsp.	0.5 mL

Combine lemon juice, olive oil and garlic in medium bowl. Add chicken. Turn until coated. Preheat electric grill for 5 minutes or gas barbecue to medium (see Note). Cook chicken on greased grill for about 5 minutes per side until no longer pink inside. Transfer to large plate. Let stand for 10 minutes. Cut into 1/8 inch (3 mm) slices. Cover to keep warm.

Cook pasta in boiling water and salt in large uncovered pot or Dutch oven for 8 to 10 minutes, stirring occasionally, until tender but firm. Drain. Rinse with cold water. Drain well. Transfer to large bowl.

(continued on next page)

Add chicken and next 4 ingredients. Toss gently.

Parsley Pesto Dressing: Process all 8 ingredients in blender or food processor until smooth. Makes about 2/3 cup (150 mL) dressing. Drizzle over salad. Toss gently. Serves 6.

1 serving: 398 Calories; 24.6 g Total Fat (13.9 g Mono, 3.3 g Poly, 5.8 g Sat); 37 mg Cholesterol; 28 g Carbohydrate; 3 g Fibre; 20 g Protein; 413 mg Sodium

Pictured below.

Note: Chicken may be broiled in the oven instead of grilled. Place chicken on a greased broiler pan. Broil on the top rack for about 5 minutes per side until no longer pink inside.

A refreshing, satisfying dish. Lovely for lunch.

variation

Instead of ham flakes, use the same amount of canned tuna. Just as tasty!

Stuffed Tomato Salad

Large tomatoes	6	6
Orzo (or other very small pasta)	1 cup	250 mL
Boiling water	6 cups	1.5 L
Salt	3/4 tsp.	4 mL
Light salad dressing (or light mayonnaise)	1/4 cup	60 mL
Grated red onion	2 tbsp.	30 mL
Prepared mustard	2 tsp.	10 mL
Chopped fresh dill (or 1/4 tsp., 1 mL, dill weed)	1 tsp.	5 mL
Pepper, sprinkle		
Can of flaked ham, drained	6 1/2 oz.	184 g
Diced celery	1/2 cup	125 mL
Diced green pepper	1/4 cup	60 mL
Jar of pimiento, well drained and chopped	2 oz.	57 mL
Green onions, chopped	2	2

Slice 1/2 inch (12 mm) from top of each tomato. Using teaspoon, carefully scoop out pulp and seeds (see Note). Invert tomatoes on large plate to drain.

Cook orzo in boiling water and salt in large uncovered saucepan, stirring occasionally, until tender but firm. Drain. Rinse with cold water. Drain well.

Combine next 5 ingredients in medium bowl.

Add orzo and remaining 5 ingredients. Stir. Spoon into each tomato. Makes 6 stuffed tomatoes.

1 stuffed tomato: 265 Calories; 6.3 g Total Fat (2.8 g Mono, 1.6 g Poly, 1.1 g Sat); 14 mg Cholesterol; 41 g Carbohydrate; 3 g Fibre; 12 g Protein; 455 mg Sodium

Pictured on page 85.

Note: Use the pulp and seeds from the tomatoes in your favourite pasta sauce recipe.

Main Macaroni Salad

Tried and true—the perfect side for a picnic or barbecue.

Elbow macaroni	2 cups	500 mL
Boiling water	8 cups	2 L
Salt	1 tsp.	5 mL
Chopped celery	3/4 cup	175 mL
Sweet pickle relish	2 tbsp.	30 mL
Grated onion (or chopped green onion)	2 tbsp.	30 mL
Large hard-cooked eggs, chopped (optional)	2	2
Salad dressing (or mayonnaise)	3/4 cup	175 mL
Salt	1 tsp.	5 mL
Pepper	1/4 tsp.	1 mL

Radish slices, for garnish

Cook macaroni in boiling water and first amount of salt in large uncovered pot or Dutch oven for 8 to 10 minutes, stirring occasionally, until tender but firm. Drain. Rinse with cold water. Drain well. Transfer to large bowl.

Add next 4 ingredients. Stir.

Combine salad dressing, second amount of salt and pepper in small bowl. Add to macaroni mixture. Stir well. Chill until cold.

Garnish with radish slices. Serves 6.

1 serving: 302 Calories; 15.9 g Total Fat (8.5 g Mono, 5.3 g Poly, 1.2 g Sat); 8 mg Cholesterol; 34 g Carbohydrate; 1 g Fibre; 5 g Protein; 648 mg Sodium

Pictured on page 89.

Shrimp Pasta Salad

Pine nuts and a dressing made with buttermilk make this salad deliciously different—the shrimp makes it company fare.

Medium bow (or other) pasta (about 7 1/2 oz., 214 g)	2 1/2 cups	625 mL
Boiling water	8 cups	2 L
Salt	1 tsp.	5 mL

(continued on next page)

Bag of frozen cooked medium shrimp (peeled and deveined), thawed	12 oz.	340 g
Finely chopped red pepper	1/2 cup	125 mL
Pine nuts, toasted (see Tip)	1/2 cup	125 mL
Finely chopped celery	1/3 cup	75 mL
Finely chopped green onion	1/4 cup	60 mL
BUTTERMILK DRESSING		
Buttermilk	1/2 cup	125 mL
Sour cream	1/4 cup	60 mL
Chopped fresh dill (or 1 1/4 tsp., 6 mL, dill weed)	1 1/2 tbsp.	25 mL
White wine vinegar	1 tbsp.	15 mL
Granulated sugar	2 tsp.	10 mL
Creamed horseradish	2 tsp.	10 mL
Salt	1/4 tsp.	1 mL
Pepper, just a pinch		

tip

To toast pine nuts, spread them in a single layer in an ungreased shallow pan. Bake in a 350°F (175°C) oven for 5 to 10 minutes, stirring or shaking often, until desired doneness.

Cook pasta in boiling water and salt in large uncovered pot or Dutch oven for 8 to 10 minutes, stirring occasionally, until tender but firm. Drain. Rinse with cold water. Drain well. Transfer to large bowl.

Add next 5 ingredients. Toss.

Buttermilk Dressing: Process all 8 ingredients in blender or food processor until smooth. Makes about 1 cup (250 mL) dressing. Drizzle over salad. Toss well. Serves 6.

1 serving: 298 Calories; 10 g Total Fat (3.3 g Mono, 3.6 g Poly, 2.4 g Sat); 115 mg Cholesterol; 33 g Carbohydrate; 4 g Fibre; 21 g Protein; 265 mg Sodium

Pictured below.

No need to toss out leftover pasta— toss it into a salad instead! A tasty blend of sweet and savoury flavours.

about dijon mustard

This strong-flavoured, pale yellow mustard gets its name from its city of origin, Dijon, France. A combination of mustard seeds, white wine and spices, Dijon mustard may be smooth, or grainy with whole seeds. French mustard labelled Dijon must adhere to strict standards. Contributing to its renowned quality are the brown mustard seeds imported from Canada. In fact, Canada provides approximately 95% of all of France's mustard needs.

Leftover Pasta Salad

Leftover cooked pasta (see Note)	1 cup	250 mL
Halved seedless green (or red) grapes	1/2 cup	125 mL
Diced medium Cheddar cheese	1/3 cup	75 mL
Diced deli ham	1/4 cup	60 mL
Sliced green onion	1 tbsp.	15 mL
CIDER DRESSING		
Mayonnaise (or salad dressing)	2 tbsp.	30 mL
Sour cream	2 tbsp.	30 mL
Dijon mustard (with whole seeds)	2 tsp.	10 mL
Apple cider vinegar	1 1/2 tsp.	7 mL
Granulated sugar	1/4 tsp.	1 mL
Salt	1/8 tsp.	0.5 mL
Pepper, sprinkle		
Dill weed, sprinkle		

Put first 5 ingredients into medium bowl. Toss.

Cider Dressing: Combine all 8 ingredients in small bowl. Chill for at least 10 minutes to blend flavours. Makes about 1/3 cup (75 mL) dressing. Drizzle over salad. Toss well. Serves 2.

1 serving: 367 Calories; 22.8 g Total Fat (9.7 g Mono, 4.7 g Poly, 7.3 g Sat); 45 mg Cholesterol; 28 g Carbohydrate; 1 g Fibre; 13 g Protein; 683 mg Sodium

Pictured on page 89.

Note: Coarsely chop long or very large pasta before measuring.

Top: Main Macaroni Salad, page 86
Bottom: Leftover Pasta Salad, above

A refreshing, Asian-style salad with a tasty peanut and lime dressing.

Peanut Rice Noodle Salad

Ingredient	Imperial	Metric
Package of small rice stick noodles (9 oz., 250 g, size)	1/2	1/2
Boiling water		
Salt	1/2 tsp.	2 mL
English cucumber (with peel), thinly sliced	1	1
Red medium pepper, julienned (see Note)	1	1
Medium carrots, julienned	2	2
Snow peas, trimmed and julienned	1 1/2 cups	375 mL
Fresh bean sprouts	1 cup	250 mL
Thinly sliced red onion	1 cup	250 mL
Large hard-cooked eggs, quartered lengthwise	6	6

PEANUT DRESSING

Ingredient	Imperial	Metric
Smooth peanut butter	1/2 cup	125 mL
Peanut (or cooking) oil	1/4 cup	60 mL
Warm water	1/4 cup	60 mL
Lime juice	3 tbsp.	50 mL
Sweet (or regular) chili sauce	2 tbsp.	30 mL
Brown sugar, packed	2 tsp.	10 mL
Fish sauce	1 tsp.	5 mL
Finely grated, peeled gingerroot (or 1/8 tsp., 0.5 mL, ground ginger)	1/2 tsp.	2 mL
Garlic clove, minced (or 1/4 tsp., 1 mL, powder)	1	1
Salted peanuts	2/3 cup	150 mL
Chopped fresh mint leaves (or 1 1/2 tsp., 7 mL, dried)	2 tbsp.	30 mL
Sesame seeds, toasted (see Tip)	1 tbsp.	15 mL

Place noodles in large heatproof bowl. Cover with boiling water. Add salt. Stir until salt is dissolved. Let stand for about 20 minutes until softened. Drain well. Transfer to extra-large bowl.

(continued on next page)

Add next 6 ingredients. Toss. Remove to large serving platter.

Arrange egg on top of noodle mixture.

Peanut Dressing: Beat first 9 ingredients with whisk in medium bowl until smooth. Makes about 1 1/3 cups (325 mL) dressing. Drizzle over salad.

Scatter remaining 3 ingredients over top. Serves 8.

1 serving: *486 Calories; 27.4 g Total Fat (12.4 g Mono, 7.6 g Poly, 5.2 g Sat); 162 mg Cholesterol; 47 g Carbohydrate; 5 g Fibre; 17 g Protein; 347 mg Sodium*

Pictured below.

Note: To julienne vegetables, cut into very thin strips that resemble matchsticks.

A lively combination of sweet and spicy ingredients. Crunchy cucumber and soft dates add an interesting texture to this zesty dish. Add extra mint to suit your taste, and serve on a bed of lettuce.

about couscous

Though it looks like rice, this staple of North African cuisine is actually tiny, pellet-like pasta made from Durum wheat semolina. While traditional cooking methods are rather complex, today's packaged versions, available in the rice section of your grocery store, are precooked and very easy to prepare. Some brands include their own seasonings or have been infused with different flavours such as tomato or garlic.

Plain couscous can be flavoured with broth, olive oil, herbs, peppers, olives, green onions—virtually anything you can think of, including fruit and nuts. Keep couscous on hand for use in salads, or to serve instead of potatoes, rice or noodles with just about anything!

Cucumber And Couscous Salad

Couscous	1 cup	250 mL
Boiling water	1 cup	250 mL
Olive (or cooking) oil	1 tbsp.	15 mL
Salt	1/4 tsp.	1 mL
Chopped English cucumber (with peel)	2 cups	500 mL
Coarsely grated zucchini (with peel)	1 cup	250 mL
Chopped pitted dates	2/3 cup	150 mL
Chopped green onion	1/2 cup	125 mL
Chopped fresh mint leaves (or 3/4 tsp., 4 mL, dried)	1 tbsp.	15 mL
CHILI DRESSING		
Olive (or cooking) oil	1/4 cup	60 mL
White wine vinegar	2 tbsp.	30 mL
Liquid honey	1 tbsp.	15 mL
Chili powder	1/2 tsp.	2 mL
Salt	1/4 tsp.	1 mL
Pepper	1/8 tsp.	0.5 mL

Combine first 4 ingredients in large heatproof bowl. Cover. Let stand for 5 minutes. Fluff with fork.

Add next 5 ingredients. Stir.

Chili Dressing: Combine all 6 ingredients in jar with tight-fitting lid. Shake well. Makes about 1/2 cup (125 mL) dressing. Drizzle over salad. Toss well. Serves 6.

1 serving: 308 Calories; 12.3 g Total Fat (8.8 g Mono, 1.1 g Poly, 1.7 g Sat); 0 mg Cholesterol; 46 g Carbohydrate; 4 g Fibre; 5 g Protein; 207 mg Sodium

Pictured on page 93.

Now this really is different. Go ahead and try it—you'll be glad you did!

Sweet Potato Salad

Cooking oil	2 tbsp.	30 mL
Reserved pineapple juice	2 tbsp.	30 mL
Lemon juice	1 tbsp.	15 mL
Salt	1/2 tsp.	2 mL
Onion salt	1/4 tsp.	1 mL
Cubed cooked, peeled sweet potato	3 cups	750 mL
Can of pineapple tidbits, drained and juice reserved	14 oz.	398 mL
Chopped celery	3/4 cup	175 mL
Slivered almonds	1/4 cup	60 mL

Combine first 5 ingredients in large bowl.

Add sweet potato. Stir until coated. Cover. Chill for at least 1 hour to blend flavours.

Add pineapple, celery and almonds. Stir. Serves 10.

1 serving: 106 Calories; 4.8 g Total Fat (2.8 g Mono, 1.3 g Poly, 0.4 g Sat); 0 mg Cholesterol; 15 g Carbohydrate; 2 g Fibre; 2 g Protein; 164 mg Sodium

Pictured on page 99.

Tabbouleh (pronounced ta-BOO-lee) comes from the Middle East. Start with a little mint and add more to taste.

variation

Although our version allows for dried herbs, only fresh herbs— and lots of them—will do for a traditional tabbouleh! To make this tabbouleh truly classic, use the larger amount of fresh mint and increase the fresh parsley to 1 cup (250 mL).

Tabbouleh

Bulgur, fine grind	1 cup	250 mL
Boiling water	1 cup	250 mL
Medium tomatoes, diced	3	3
Green onions, chopped	3	3
Olive (or cooking) oil	1/4 cup	60 mL
Lemon juice	2 tbsp.	30 mL
Chopped fresh mint leaves (or 3/4 – 1 1/2 tsp., 4 – 7 mL, dried)	1 – 2 tbsp.	15 – 30 mL
Finely chopped fresh parsley (or 1/4 tsp., 1 mL, flakes)	1 1/2 tsp.	7 mL
Salt	1 tsp.	5 mL
Pepper	1/4 tsp.	1 mL
Ground allspice	1/8 tsp.	0.5 mL

(continued on next page)

Measure bulgur into large heatproof bowl. Add boiling water. Cover. Let stand for about 15 minutes until water is absorbed.

Add remaining 9 ingredients. Stir well. Serves 4.

1 serving: 277 Calories; 15.2 g Total Fat (10.7 g Mono, 1.5 g Poly, 2.1 g Sat); 0 mg Cholesterol; 33 g Carbohydrate; 5 g Fibre; 5 g Protein; 609 mg Sodium

Pictured below.

Fresh mint and cashews add an unexpected flair to this potato salad. The light, slightly sweet dressing will have them asking for more.

tip

To toast cashews, spread them in a single layer in an ungreased shallow pan. Bake in a 350°F (175°C) oven for 5 to 10 minutes, stirring or shaking often, until desired doneness.

Potato Mint Salad

Red medium potatoes (with skin), about 3 lbs. (1.4 kg)	6	6
Water		
Finely chopped red pepper	1/2 cup	125 mL
Raw cashews, toasted (see Tip), optional	3 tbsp.	50 mL
CREAMY MINT DRESSING		
Sour cream	1/2 cup	125 mL
Coarsely chopped fresh mint leaves	1/4 cup	60 mL
Liquid honey	2 tbsp.	30 mL
Lemon juice	2 tbsp.	30 mL
Dry mustard	2 tsp.	10 mL
Salt	1/2 tsp.	2 mL
Pepper	1/2 tsp.	2 mL
Chopped fresh chives (optional)	2 tbsp.	30 mL

Cook whole potatoes in water in large pot or Dutch oven until just tender. Drain. Let stand until cool enough to handle. Cut each potato in half lengthwise. Cut each half crosswise into 1/2 inch (12 mm) slices. Put into large bowl.

Add red pepper and cashews. Stir.

Creamy Mint Dressing: Process first 7 ingredients in blender or food processor until smooth. Makes about 3/4 cup (175 mL) dressing. Drizzle over salad. Stir well.

Sprinkle with chives. Serves 6.

1 serving: 174 Calories; 3.4 g Total Fat (1.1 g Mono, 0.3 g Poly, 1.8 g Sat); 8 mg Cholesterol; 33 g Carbohydrate; 3 g Fibre; 4 g Protein; 218 mg Sodium

Pictured on page 97.

A time-honoured classic and one of the best.

about potatoes

The many varieties of potatoes are categorized by their best use: baking, boiling and all-purpose. Baking potatoes, higher in starch than moisture, are dry and mealy when baked and are best used for mashed potato salads. Boiling potatoes, higher in moisture than starch, hold their shape when boiled—excellent for cutting up for potato salads. All-purpose potatoes are somewhere in-between.

Potato Salad

Cubed cooked, peeled potato	6 cups	1.5 L
Large hard-cooked eggs, chopped	4	4
Chopped celery	1 cup	250 mL
Sliced radish	1/4 cup	60 mL
Green onions, chopped	4	4
Chopped fresh parsley (or 1 tsp., 5 mL, flakes)	1 1/2 tbsp.	25 mL
Salad dressing (or mayonnaise)	1 cup	250 mL
Milk	1/4 cup	60 mL
Apple cider vinegar	1 tbsp.	15 mL
Granulated sugar	2 tsp.	10 mL
Prepared mustard	1 tsp.	5 mL
Salt	1 1/2 tsp.	7 mL
Pepper	1/4 tsp.	1 mL
Onion powder	1/4 tsp.	1 mL

Paprika, sprinkle
Sprig of fresh dill, for garnish

Put first 6 ingredients into large bowl. Stir.

Combine next 8 ingredients in small bowl. Drizzle over salad. Stir well. Cover. Chill for at least 2 hours to blend flavours.

Sprinkle with paprika. Garnish with dill. Serves 10.

1 serving: 250 Calories; 14.5 g Total Fat (7.6 g Mono, 4.4 g Poly, 1.6 g Sat); 93 mg Cholesterol; 25 g Carbohydrate; 2 g Fibre; 5 g Protein; 563 mg Sodium

Pictured on page 99.

This salad is a perfect way to use up leftover mashed potatoes, and a great reason to plan a picnic for two!

Mashed Potato Salad

Large hard-cooked egg, chopped	1	1
Salad dressing (or mayonnaise)	1/3 cup	75 mL
Diced celery	1/4 cup	60 mL
Green onion, sliced	1	1
Sweet pickle relish	2 tsp.	10 mL
Onion powder	1/8 tsp.	0.5 mL
Salt	1/8 tsp.	0.5 mL

(continued on next page)

Mashed potatoes	1 cup	250 mL
Large hard-cooked egg, sliced	1	1
Paprika, sprinkle		

Combine first 7 ingredients in medium bowl.

Add mashed potatoes. Stir. Remove to small serving bowl.

Arrange egg slices on top of salad. Sprinkle with paprika. Cover. Chill for 1 hour to blend flavours. Serves 2.

1 serving: 409 Calories; 25.7 g Total Fat (13.2 g Mono, 7.5 g Poly, 3.1 g Sat); 226 mg Cholesterol; 36 g Carbohydrate; 2 g Fibre; 9 g Protein; 535 mg Sodium

Pictured below.

Top: Potato Salad, page 98
Bottom Right: Sweet Potato Salad, page 94
Bottom Left: Mashed Potato Salad, page 98

You'll love the mild curry vinaigrette in this salad. It perfectly complements the shrimp and rice.

Best Rice Salad

Cold cooked rice (about 2/3 cup, 150 mL, uncooked), see Note	2 cups	500 mL
Chopped celery	1 1/2 cups	375 mL
Fresh (or frozen, thawed) peas	1 cup	250 mL
Can of small shrimp, drained	4 oz.	113 g
Finely chopped green onion	1/4 cup	60 mL
CURRY VINAIGRETTE		
Cooking (or olive) oil	1/2 cup	125 mL
White vinegar	3 tbsp.	50 mL
Soy sauce	2 tbsp.	30 mL
Curry powder	1 1/2 – 2 tsp.	7 – 10 mL
Granulated sugar	1/2 tsp.	2 mL
Celery salt	1/2 tsp.	2 mL

Combine first 5 ingredients in large bowl.

Curry Vinaigrette: Combine all 6 ingredients in jar with tight-fitting lid. Shake well. Makes about 7/8 cup (200 mL) dressing. Drizzle over salad. Stir gently. Serves 4 to 6.

1 serving: 465 Calories; 29.7 g Total Fat (17.1 g Mono, 8.8 g Poly, 2.2 g Sat); 23 mg Cholesterol; 41 g Carbohydrate; 1 g Fibre; 10 g Protein; 740 mg Sodium

Note: For added flavour, use brown or jasmine rice.

Italian Hot Potato Salad

A quick and easy-to-make hot potato salad with an Italian flair.

Bacon slices, diced	6	6
Cubed cooked potato	4 cups	1 L
Green onions, sliced	4	4
Chopped celery	1/2 cup	125 mL
Italian dressing	1/2 cup	125 mL
Grated Parmesan cheese	1/2 cup	125 mL

(continued on next page)

Cook bacon in large frying pan until crisp. Transfer with slotted spoon to paper towels to drain. Set aside. Discard drippings, reserving about 1 tsp. (5 mL) in pan.

Heat drippings on medium. Add next 4 ingredients. Heat and stir for about 8 minutes until heated through. Transfer to large bowl.

Add bacon and Parmesan cheese. Stir. Serve immediately. Serves 4.

1 serving: 438 Calories; 30.3 g Total Fat (15.3 g Mono, 7.9 g Poly, 5.7 g Sat); 39 mg Cholesterol; 32 g Carbohydrate; 3 g Fibre; 12 g Protein; 911 mg Sodium

Pictured below.

A great way to use up leftover rice and veggies. Stuff this salad into a pita pocket for a tasty sandwich.

variation

For extra goodness, add 2 tbsp. (30 mL) sunflower seeds or shelled pumpkin seeds, or add up to 1/4 cup (60 mL) raisins.

Rice Salad

Cold cooked rice (about 1/4 cup, 60 mL, uncooked)	3/4 cup	175 mL
Cold cooked vegetables (such as peas, broccoli florets or green beans)	1/2 cup	125 mL
Chopped cooked ham	1/3 cup	75 mL
Grated carrot	1/4 cup	60 mL
Sliced green onion	2 tbsp.	30 mL
White vinegar (see Note)	2 tsp.	10 mL
Olive (or cooking) oil	1 tsp.	5 mL
Salt, sprinkle		

Combine all 8 ingredients in small bowl. Serves 2.

1 serving: 198 Calories; 4.9 g Total Fat (2.9 g Mono, 0.7 g Poly, 1.2 g Sat); 14 mg Cholesterol; 29 g Carbohydrate; 2 g Fibre; 9 g Protein; 380 mg Sodium

Pictured on page 103.

Note: If preferred, use the same amount of white wine vinegar or apple cider vinegar instead of white vinegar.

Bright, crispy vegetables together with rice and pineapple in one delicious salad. Coconut adds the final tropical touch!

Crunchy Rice Salad

Cold cooked long grain white rice (about 2/3 cup, 150 mL, uncooked), see Note	2 cups	500 mL
Can of pineapple tidbits, drained	14 oz.	398 mL
Can of sliced water chestnuts, drained and chopped	8 oz.	227 mL
Diced celery	1/2 cup	125 mL
Diced red pepper	1/2 cup	125 mL
Diced red onion	1/2 cup	125 mL
LIME DRESSING		
Lime juice	3 tbsp.	50 mL
Cooking (or olive) oil	1 tbsp.	15 mL
Low-sodium soy sauce	1 tbsp.	15 mL
Sweet chili sauce	1 tbsp.	15 mL

(continued on next page)

Shredded (long thread) or flake coconut,   1/4 cup   60 mL
   toasted (see Tip), optional

Combine first 6 ingredients in large bowl.

Lime Dressing: Combine first 4 ingredients in jar with tight-fitting lid. Shake well. Makes about 1/3 cup (75 mL) dressing. Drizzle over salad. Stir.

Sprinkle with coconut. Serves 6.

1 serving: 172 Calories; 2.7 g Total Fat (1.4 g Mono, 0.8 g Poly, 0.2 g Sat); 0 mg Cholesterol; 34 g Carbohydrate; 2 g Fibre; 3 g Protein; 134 mg Sodium

Pictured below.

Note: For an authentic Asian flavour, use jasmine or basmati rice.

tip

To toast coconut, spread in a single layer in an ungreased shallow pan. Bake in a 350°F (175°C) oven for 5 to 10 minutes, stirring or shaking often, until desired doneness.

Top: Crunchy Rice Salad, page 102
Bottom Left and Bottom Right: Rice Salad, page 102

A basic oil and vinegar dressing that's delicious on any combination of salad greens and vegetables.

Vinaigrette

Olive (or cooking) oil	6 tbsp.	100 mL
Apple cider (or red wine) vinegar	3 tbsp.	50 mL
Granulated sugar	1 tsp.	5 mL
Paprika	1/2 tsp.	2 mL
Onion salt	1/4 tsp.	1 mL
Pepper, sprinkle		

Combine all 6 ingredients in jar with tight-fitting lid. Shake well. Store in refrigerator for up to 2 weeks. Shake well before drizzling over salad. Makes about 1/2 cup (125 mL).

2 tbsp. (30 mL): 180 Calories; 19.7 g Total Fat (14.5 g Mono, 1.7 g Poly, 2.7 g Sat); 0 mg Cholesterol; 2 g Carbohydrate; 0 g Fibre; 0 g Protein; 74 mg Sodium

Pictured on page 105.

Great for tossing with mixed greens or for marinating vegetables.

storing olive oil

Olive oil is best stored in a cool, dark place, where it will keep for up to 6 months. It may be stored in the refrigerator for up to a year, but will become cloudy and too thick to pour. Room temperature will return it to a clear liquid, but we suggest you buy only as much as you will use in a short time.

Italian Dressing

Cooking (or olive) oil	1 cup	250 mL
Lemon juice	1/4 cup	60 mL
White vinegar	1/4 cup	60 mL
Granulated sugar	2 tsp.	10 mL
Salt	1 tsp.	5 mL
Garlic salt	1/2 tsp.	2 mL
Onion salt	1/2 tsp.	2 mL
Dry mustard	1/2 tsp.	2 mL
Paprika	1/2 tsp.	2 mL
Dried oregano	1/2 tsp.	2 mL
Ground thyme	1/8 tsp.	0.5 mL

Combine all 11 ingredients in jar with tight-fitting lid. Shake well. Chill for 2 hours to blend flavours. Store in refrigerator for up to 2 weeks. Shake well before drizzling over salad. Makes about 1 1/2 cups (375 mL).

2 tbsp. (30 mL): 169 Calories; 18.5 g Total Fat (10.9 g Mono, 5.5 g Poly, 1.3 g Sat); 0 mg Cholesterol; 2 g Carbohydrate; 0 g Fibre; 0 g Protein; 285 mg Sodium

Pictured on page 105.

Photo legend
1. Italian Dressing, above
2. French Dressing, page 106
3. Cooked Salad Dressing, page 106
4. Vinaigrette, above
5. Blue Cheese Dressing, page 107

A favourite from way, way back. With the consistency of mayonnaise, this thick, tangy dressing is best for potato salads, coleslaws, chunky vegetable or pasta salads, or salads made with iceberg lettuce.

Cooked Salad Dressing

Granulated sugar	1/2 cup	125 mL
All-purpose flour	2 tbsp.	30 mL
Dry mustard	1 tbsp.	15 mL
Salt	1 tsp.	5 mL
Large eggs	3	3
Milk	1 cup	250 mL
White vinegar	1/2 cup	125 mL
Water	1/2 cup	125 mL

Combine first 4 ingredients in heavy medium saucepan. Add eggs 1 at a time, beating well after each addition.

Add milk, vinegar and water. Heat and stir on medium for 10 to 12 minutes until boiling and thickened. Cool slightly. Transfer to airtight container. Store in refrigerator for up to 3 weeks. Stir well before adding to salad. Makes about 2 1/2 cups (625 mL).

2 tbsp. (30 mL): 42 Calories; 1 g Total Fat (0.4 g Mono, 0.1 g Poly, 0.3 g Sat); 32 mg Cholesterol; 7 g Carbohydrate; 0 g Fibre; 2 g Protein; 129 mg Sodium

Pictured on page 105.

A tasty red dressing for your favourite tossed salad.

French Dressing

Can of condensed tomato soup	10 oz.	284 mL
Chopped onion	1/3 cup	75 mL
Apple cider vinegar	1/4 cup	60 mL
Granulated sugar	1/4 cup	60 mL
Cooking oil	3 tbsp.	50 mL
Worcestershire sauce	3/4 tsp.	4 mL
Garlic clove, minced (or 1/4 tsp., 1 mL, powder)	1	1
Salt	1/4 tsp.	1 mL

Process all 8 ingredients in blender or food processor until smooth. Pour into jar with tight-fitting lid. Store in refrigerator for up to 1 week. Shake well before drizzling over salad. Makes about 2 cups (500 mL).

2 tbsp. (30 mL): 49 Calories; 2.8 g Total Fat (1.5 g Mono, 0.9 g Poly, 0.2 g Sat); 0 mg Cholesterol; 6 g Carbohydrate; 0 g Fibre; 0 g Protein; 164 mg Sodium

Pictured on page 105.

Blue Cheese Dressing

Light mayonnaise (or light salad dressing)	1 cup	250 mL
Crumbled blue cheese (about 4 oz.,113 g)	3/4 cup	175 mL
Light sour cream	1/2 cup	125 mL
White vinegar	1 tbsp.	15 mL
Seasoned salt	1 tsp.	5 mL
Salt	1/2 tsp.	2 mL
Pepper	1/4 tsp.	1 mL
Onion powder	1/4 tsp.	1 mL
Garlic clove, minced (or 1/4 tsp., 1 mL, powder)	1	1
Milk (optional)	2 tbsp.	30 mL

Process first 9 ingredients in blender or food processor until smooth.

Add milk. Process until just combined. Pour into jar with tight-fitting lid. Store in refrigerator for up to 1 week. Shake well before drizzling over salad. Makes about 2 cups (500 mL).

2 tbsp. (30 mL): 77 Calories; 7.1 g Total Fat (3.5 g Mono, 1.5 g Poly, 2.2 g Sat); 7 mg Cholesterol; 2 g Carbohydrate; 0 g Fibre; 2 g Protein; 340 mg Sodium

Pictured on page 105.

Blue cheese lovers will enjoy the tangy, pungent flavour of this one. Add or omit the milk depending on how thick you like your dressing. Delicious on mixed greens, or try it in potato salad.

Dijon Dressing

Olive (or cooking) oil	1/4 cup	60 mL
Dijon mustard	2 tbsp.	30 mL
Mayonnaise (or salad dressing)	1 tbsp.	15 mL
Red wine vinegar	1 tbsp.	15 mL
Lemon juice	1 tbsp.	15 mL
Brown sugar, packed	1 tsp.	5 mL
Salt	1/4 tsp.	1 mL

Combine all 7 ingredients in jar with tight-fitting lid. Shake well. Store in refrigerator for up to 1 week. Shake well before drizzling over salad. Makes about 1/2 cup (125 mL).

2 tbsp. (30 mL): 159 Calories; 17 g Total Fat (11.7 g Mono, 2.4 g Poly, 2.2 g Sat); 2 mg Cholesterol; 2 g Carbohydrate; 0 g Fibre; 1 g Protein; 260 mg Sodium

Pictured on page 109.

Dijon mustard is a classic flavouring in salad dressings and vinaigrettes. This one will add a zesty flavour to your mixed green salads. Also good used in a marinated veggie salad.

As an alternative to Caesar flavours, dress your romaine lettuce salad in this creamy dressing. A nice dressing for pasta salads, too!

Creamy Garlic Dressing

Light salad dressing (or light mayonnaise)	1/2 cup	125 mL
Milk	1/4 cup	60 mL
White vinegar	2 tsp.	10 mL
Garlic cloves, minced (or 1 tsp., 5 mL, powder)	4	4
Granulated sugar	1/2 tsp.	2 mL
Dry mustard	1/4 tsp.	1 mL
Onion powder	1/8 tsp.	0.5 mL
Salt	1/8 tsp.	0.5 mL
Pepper, sprinkle		

Combine all 9 ingredients in small bowl. Transfer to airtight container. Store in refrigerator for up to 1 week. Stir well before drizzling over salad. Makes about 3/4 cup (175 mL).

2 tbsp. (30 mL): 67 Calories; 5.2 g Total Fat (3 g Mono, 1.5 g Poly, 0.3 g Sat); 0 mg Cholesterol; 5 g Carbohydrate; 0 g Fibre; 1 g Protein; 208 mg Sodium

Pictured on page 109.

Also known as "Italian Vinaigrette," this dressing is delicious tossed with a mixture of salad greens and tomatoes.

tip

To reduce the fat content of any salad, simply use less dressing. Add just enough to flavour greens.

Martini Dressing

Olive (or cooking) oil	2/3 cup	150 mL
White wine vinegar	6 tbsp.	100 mL
Grated Romano cheese	6 tbsp.	100 mL
Chopped fresh basil	1/4 cup	60 mL
Garlic cloves	6	6

Process all 5 ingredients in blender or food processor for about 1 minute until well combined. Pour into jar with tight-fitting lid. Store in refrigerator for up to 1 week. Shake well before drizzling over salad. Makes about 1 cup (250 mL).

2 tbsp. (30 mL): 185 Calories; 19.6 g Total Fat (13.9 g Mono, 1.6 g Poly, 3.3 g Sat); 5 mg Cholesterol; 2 g Carbohydrate; 0 g Fibre; 2 g Protein; 55 mg Sodium

Pictured on page 109.

Clockwise from Centre Left:
Dijon Dressing, page 107
Martini Dressing, above
Creamy Garlic Dressing, above

Thick and pleasantly pink. A delectable complement to a spinach and fruit salad.

about vinaigrette

The standard ratio for basic vinaigrette—three parts oil to one part vinegar—is a good starting point when creating your own, however the ratio may be changed to suit personal taste. Experiment, using olive or cooking oil and vinegars such as red or white wine, apple cider or balsamic. Season with fresh herbs and spices, and let nothing but your imagination stop you!

Apple cider vinegar provides a fruity taste to this delicious vinaigrette. Great drizzled over a mixture of greens and cut-up fresh fruit.

Poppy Seed Dressing

Granulated sugar	3/4 cup	175 mL
White vinegar	1/3 cup	75 mL
Dry mustard	1 tsp.	5 mL
Onion flakes	1 tsp.	5 mL
Salt	1 tsp.	5 mL
Cooking oil	1 cup	250 mL
Poppy seeds	1 1/2 tbsp.	25 mL
Drop of red liquid food colouring	1	1

Process first 5 ingredients in blender or food processor until smooth.

With motor running, add cooking oil in thin stream through hole in lid until thickened. Pour into jar with tight-fitting lid.

Add poppy seeds and food colouring. Shake well. Store in refrigerator for up to 3 weeks. Shake well before drizzling over salad. Makes about 1 2/3 cups (400 mL).

2 tbsp. (30 mL): 197 Calories; 17 g Total Fat (9.8 g Mono, 5.2 g Poly, 1.2 g Sat); 0 mg Cholesterol; 12 g Carbohydrate; 0 g Fibre; 0 g Protein; 170 mg Sodium

Pictured on page 111.

Apple Cider Vinaigrette

Cooking oil	6 tbsp.	100 mL
Apple cider vinegar	2 tbsp.	30 mL
Granulated sugar	1 tsp.	5 mL
Dry mustard	1 tsp.	5 mL
Garlic clove, minced (or 1/4 tsp., 1 mL, powder)	1	1
Salt	1 tsp.	5 mL
Pepper	1/2 tsp.	2 mL

Combine all 7 ingredients in jar with tight-fitting lid. Shake well. Store in refrigerator for up to 1 week. Shake well before drizzling over salad. Makes about 1/2 cup (125 mL).

2 tbsp. (30 mL): 186 Calories; 20.1 g Total Fat (11.9 g Mono, 5.9 g Poly, 1.4 g Sat); 0 mg Cholesterol; 2 g Carbohydrate; 0 g Fibre; 0 g Protein; 569 mg Sodium

Pictured on page 111.

Pink Dressing

Salad dressing (or mayonnaise)	1 cup	250 mL
Pineapple tidbits, drained	1 cup	250 mL
Granulated sugar	1/4 cup	60 mL
Chopped walnuts	1/4 cup	60 mL
Maraschino cherry syrup	1/4 cup	60 mL
Chopped maraschino cherries	1/4 cup	60 mL
Whipping cream	1/4 cup	60 mL

Process first 6 ingredients in blender or food processor until smooth. Transfer to medium bowl.

Beat whipping cream in small bowl until stiff peaks form. Fold into pineapple mixture. Transfer to airtight container. Store in refrigerator for up to 1 week. Stir well before drizzling over salad. Makes about 2 cups (500 mL).

2 tbsp. (30 mL): 124 Calories; 9.7 g Total Fat (4.7 g Mono, 3.2 g Poly, 1.4 g Sat); 8 mg Cholesterol; 9 g Carbohydrate; trace Fibre; 1 g Protein; 95 mg Sodium

Pictured below.

A delicious dressing to mix with fresh fruit or to spoon over spinach or lettuce leaves. Use it as a fruit dip, too!

Clockwise from Top Left:
Apple Cider Vinaigrette, page 110
Pink Dressing, above
Poppy Seed Dressing, page 110

Invigorate your favourite Asian-style salads with this tangy dressing.

about sesame oil

Sesame oil has a deep amber colour and a rich, nutty flavour. Because of its intense flavour, sesame oil is generally used in small amounts.

Ginger Dressing

Slice of gingerroot (1/2 inch, 12 mm, thick), peeled	1	1
Green onion, cut into 4 pieces	1	1
Baby carrot, halved	1	1
Garlic clove, minced (or 1/4 tsp., 1 mL, powder)	1	1
Cooking oil	1/2 cup	125 mL
Rice vinegar	1/3 cup	75 mL
Soy sauce	1 tbsp.	15 mL
Dry mustard	1/2 tsp.	2 mL
Sesame oil, for flavour (optional)	2 tsp.	10 mL

Process all 9 ingredients in blender or food processor for about 1 minute, scraping down sides if necessary, until smooth. Pour into jar with tight-fitting lid. Chill for 1 hour to blend flavours. Store in refrigerator for up to 1 week. Shake well before drizzling over salad. Makes about 1 cup (250 mL).

2 tbsp. (30 mL): 128 Calories; 13.9 g Total Fat (8.2 g Mono, 4.1 g Poly, 1 g Sat); 0 mg Cholesterol; 1 g Carbohydrate; 0 g Fibre; 0 g Protein; 126 mg Sodium

Pictured on page 113.

A sweet, fragrant dressing with a ginger and chili bite. Perfect tossed with dark leafy greens, or used as a dipping sauce for meatballs or chicken.

tip

To toast sesame seeds, spread them in a single layer in an ungreased shallow pan. Bake in a 350°F (175°C) oven for 5 to 10 minutes, stirring or shaking often, until desired doneness.

Sesame Soy Dressing

White vinegar	1/3 cup	75 mL
Indonesian sweet (or thick) soy sauce	1/4 cup	60 mL
Finely grated, peeled gingerroot (or 3/4 tsp., 4 mL, ground ginger)	1 tbsp.	15 mL
Brown sugar, packed	1 tbsp.	15 mL
Sesame seeds, toasted (see Tip)	1 tbsp.	15 mL
Sesame oil, for flavour	2 tsp.	10 mL
Dried crushed chilies	1/2 tsp.	2 mL
Cooking oil	1/4 cup	60 mL

(continued on next page)

Process first 7 ingredients in blender or food processor for about 5 seconds until foamy.

With motor running, add cooking oil in thin stream through hole in lid until well combined. Pour into jar with tight-fitting lid. Store in refrigerator for up to 1 week. Shake well before drizzling over salad. Makes about 1 cup (250 mL).

2 tbsp. (30 mL): 91 Calories; 8.7 g Total Fat (4.8 g Mono, 2.8 g Poly, 0.7 g Sat); 0 mg Cholesterol; 3 g Carbohydrate; trace Fibre; 1 g Protein; 417 mg Sodium

Pictured below.

Top: Ginger Dressing, page 112
Bottom: Sesame Soy Dressing, page 112

Only two ingredients, and low-fat, too! Toss it with orange segments in your favourite green salad, or add it to a fruit salad for a zesty finish.

Tangy Orange Dressing

| Light salad dressing (or light mayonnaise) | 2/3 cup | 150 mL |
| Frozen concentrated orange juice, thawed | 1/3 cup | 75 mL |

Combine salad dressing and concentrated orange juice in small bowl. Transfer to airtight container. Store in refrigerator for up to 1 week. Stir well before drizzling over salad. Makes about 1 cup (250 mL).

2 tbsp. (30 mL): 76 Calories; 5.1 g Total Fat (2.9 g Mono, 1.5 g Poly, 0.3 g Sat); 0 mg Cholesterol; 8 g Carbohydrate; trace Fibre; 0 g Protein; 154 mg Sodium

Pictured on page 115.

Fresh and light—perfect on delicate baby greens. Tangy and fruity, with no added fat!

Raspberry Dressing

Fresh (or frozen, thawed) raspberries	3 cups	750 mL
White vinegar	1 cup	250 mL
Granulated sugar	1 1/2 cups	375 mL

Combine raspberries and vinegar in small bowl. Cover. Chill for 48 hours.

Transfer raspberry mixture to medium saucepan. Add sugar. Stir. Bring to a boil on medium, stirring often. Reduce heat to medium-low. Simmer, uncovered, for 15 minutes without stirring. Cool slightly. Press raspberry mixture through sieve into medium bowl. Discard seeds. Pour into jar with tight-fitting lid. Store in refrigerator for up to 1 month. Shake well before drizzling over salad. Makes about 2 cups (500 mL).

2 tbsp. (30 mL): 87 Calories; 0.1 g Total Fat (0 g Mono, 0.1 g Poly, 0 g Sat); 0 mg Cholesterol; 22 g Carbohydrate; 1 g Fibre; 0 g Protein; 0 mg Sodium

Pictured on page 115.

Clockwise from top left:
Honey Mustard Dressing, page 116
Raspberry Dressing, above
Tangy Orange Dressing, above
Cucumber Dressing, page 116
Thousand Island Dressing, page 117

A perfect blend of tangy and sweet flavours. This low-fat dressing adds lots of flavour to mixed greens.

Honey Mustard Dressing

Liquid honey	1/4 cup	60 mL
White vinegar	1/4 cup	60 mL
Prepared mustard	2 tsp.	10 mL
Cornstarch	2 tsp.	10 mL

Combine all 4 ingredients in small saucepan. Heat and stir on medium for about 8 minutes until boiling and thickened. Cool. Pour into jar with tight-fitting lid. Store in refrigerator for up to 1 week. Shake well before drizzling over salad. Makes about 1/2 cup (125 mL).

2 tbsp. (30 mL): 87 Calories; 0.2 g Total Fat (0 g Mono, 0.1 g Poly, 0 g Sat); 0 mg Cholesterol; 23 g Carbohydrate; 0 g Fibre; 0 g Protein; 39 mg Sodium

Pictured on page 115.

Cool cucumber and dill dressing is a great choice any time. Makes a nice dip for vegetable sticks, too!

Cucumber Dressing

Diced peeled English cucumber	1/2 cup	125 mL
Sour cream	1/3 cup	75 mL
Lemon juice	1 tsp.	5 mL
Chopped fresh parsley (or 1/4 tsp., 1 mL, flakes)	1 tsp.	5 mL
Chopped fresh dill (or 1/4 tsp., 1 mL, dill weed)	1 tsp.	5 mL
Salt	1/4 tsp.	1 mL

Combine all 6 ingredients in small bowl. Transfer to airtight container. Store in refrigerator for up to 1 week. Stir well before drizzling over salad. Makes about 3/4 cup (175 mL).

2 tbsp. (30 mL): 21 Calories; 1.8 g Total Fat (0.5 g Mono, 0.1 g Poly, 1.1 g Sat); 5 mg Cholesterol; 1 g Carbohydrate; 0 g Fibre; 0 g Protein; 100 mg Sodium

Pictured on page 115.

Thousand Island Dressing

Salad dressing (or mayonnaise)	3/4 cup	175 mL
Chili sauce	1/3 cup	75 mL
Sweet pickle relish	2 1/2 tbsp.	37 mL
Finely chopped onion	2 tsp.	10 mL
Large hard-cooked egg, chopped	1	1
Chopped pimiento	2 tsp.	10 mL

Combine first 4 ingredients in medium bowl.

Add egg and pimiento. Stir. Transfer to airtight container. Store in refrigerator for up to 2 days. Stir well before drizzling over salad. Makes about 1 1/3 cups (325 mL).

2 tbsp. (30 mL): 104 Calories; 8.8 g Total Fat (4.7 g Mono, 2.8 g Poly, 0.8 g Sat); 24 mg Cholesterol; 7 g Carbohydrate; trace Fibre; 1 g Protein; 254 mg Sodium

Pictured on page 115.

Always a favourite. Put a ladle in a bowl of this dressing and let guests help themselves.

Roasted Pecans

Hard margarine (or butter)	1 tbsp.	15 mL
Pecan halves	2 cups	500 mL
Worcestershire sauce	2 tbsp.	30 mL
Ketchup	2 tsp.	10 mL
Cayenne pepper	1/4 tsp.	1 mL

Salt, sprinkle

Melt margarine in large saucepan. Add next 4 ingredients. Stir until pecans are coated. Spread evenly in greased baking sheet with sides. Bake in 350°F (175°C) oven for 20 minutes, stirring every 5 minutes. Transfer to separate paper towel-lined baking sheet.

Sprinkle with salt. Cool. Store in airtight container at room temperature for up to 2 weeks. Makes about 2 cups (500 mL).

1/4 cup (60 mL): 206 Calories; 20.8 g Total Fat (13 g Mono, 4.9 g Poly, 1.9 g Sat); 0 mg Cholesterol; 6 g Carbohydrate; 2 g Fibre; 3 g Protein; 71 mg Sodium

When money is no object, these pecans turn a salad into a celebration.

This sweet and spicy nut mix is sure to please. Sprinkle it over fruit and spinach salads for a sweet, crunchy finish.

Spiced Nuts

Brown sugar, packed	1/2 cup	125 mL
Granulated sugar	1/2 cup	125 mL
Ground cinnamon	1 1/2 tsp.	7 mL
Ground nutmeg	1/2 tsp.	2 mL
Ground ginger	1/2 tsp.	2 mL
Ground cloves	1/4 tsp.	1 mL
Egg white (large)	1	1
Water	1 tbsp.	15 mL
Mixed nuts	4 cups	1 L

Combine first 6 ingredients in small bowl.

Beat egg white and water in medium bowl until frothy. Add brown sugar mixture. Stir well.

Add nuts. Stir until coated. Spread evenly in greased baking sheet with sides. Bake in 325°F (160°C) oven for about 20 minutes, stirring occasionally, until golden. Cool. Store in airtight container at room temperature for up to 2 weeks. Makes about 6 cups (1.5 L).

1/4 cup (60 mL): 180 Calories; 12.4 g Total Fat (7.6 g Mono, 2.6 g Poly, 1.7 g Sat); 0 mg Cholesterol; 15 g Carbohydrate; 1 g Fibre; 4 g Protein; 7 mg Sodium

Pictured on page 119.

Sprinkle this savoury mixture on a green leaf or noodle salad. Goes great with Ginger Dressing, page 112.

Sesame Walnut Topping

Finely chopped walnuts	2 tbsp.	30 mL
Sesame seeds	1 tbsp.	15 mL
Cumin seed	1/2 tsp.	2 mL

Heat and stir all 3 ingredients in small frying pan on medium for about 3 minutes until fragrant. Transfer to small custard cup. Cool. Store in airtight container at room temperature for up to 2 weeks. Makes about 3 tbsp. (50 mL).

1 tsp. (5 mL): 13 Calories; 1.2 g Total Fat (0.3 g Mono, 0.7 g Poly, 0.1 g Sat); 0 mg Cholesterol; 0 g Carbohydrate; trace Fibre; 0 g Protein; 0 mg Sodium

Pictured on page 119.

Clockwise from Top Left:
Spiced Nuts, above
Basil Pesto Croutons, page 120
Sesame Walnut Topping, above

Beat the crouton blahs with these savoury morsels! Scatter them over your favourite tossed salad for a flavourful finishing crunch.

tomato pesto croutons

Instead of basil pesto, use the same amount of sun-dried tomato pesto.

Basil Pesto Croutons

Basil pesto	2 tbsp.	30 mL
Peanut (or cooking) oil	1 tbsp.	15 mL
Small dry bread cubes	1 cup	250 mL

Combine pesto and peanut oil in medium bowl. Add bread cubes. Toss until coated. Spread evenly in greased baking sheet with sides. Bake in 375°F (190°C) oven for about 10 minutes, stirring once, until golden and crisp. Cool. Store in airtight container at room temperature for up to 1 week. Makes about 1 cup (250 mL).

1/4 cup (60 mL): 75 Calories; 6.1 g Total Fat (3.4 g Mono, 1.4 g Poly, 1 g Sat); 0 mg Cholesterol; 5 g Carbohydrate; trace Fibre; 1 g Protein; 50 mg Sodium

Pictured on page 119.

These crispy, flavourful crackers are a cinch to make. A great way to encourage kids to eat their salad!

Little Dilled Snacks

Hard margarine (or butter)	1/2 cup	125 mL
Envelope of ranch dressing mix (1 oz., 28 g), stir before measuring	1/2	1/2
Chopped fresh dill (or 1 1/2 tsp., 7 mL, dill weed)	2 tbsp.	30 mL
Paprika	1/4 tsp.	1 mL
Plain-flavoured fish-shaped crackers	4 cups	1 L

Melt margarine in medium saucepan. Add dressing mix, dill and paprika. Stir well.

Put crackers into large bowl. Drizzle with dill mixture. Toss until coated. Spread evenly in ungreased baking sheet with sides. Bake in 300°F (150°C) oven for about 15 minutes, stirring after 10 minutes, until crisp and golden. Cool. Store in airtight container at room temperature for up to 2 weeks. Makes about 4 cups (1 L).

1/4 cup (60 mL): 124 Calories; 9.4 g Total Fat (5.4 g Mono, 1.7 g Poly, 1.9 g Sat); 0 mg Cholesterol; 9 g Carbohydrate; trace Fibre; 1 g Protein; 308 mg Sodium

Pictured on page 121.

Minted Pita Chips

Finely chopped fresh mint leaves (or 1 1/2 tsp., 7 mL, dried)	2 tbsp.	30 mL
Olive (or cooking) oil	2 tbsp.	30 mL
Sesame seeds, toasted (see Tip)	2 tsp.	10 mL
Poppy seeds	2 tsp.	10 mL
Salt	1/8 tsp.	0.5 mL
Pita breads (7 inch, 18 cm, diameter), split	3	3

Combine first 5 ingredients in small bowl.

Place pita bread rounds, inside-up, on greased baking sheet. Brush with mint mixture. Bake in 350°F (175°C) oven for about 10 minutes until crisp and golden. Cool. Break into irregular-shaped pieces, 2 to 3 inches (5 to 7.5 cm) each. Store in airtight container at room temperature for up to 2 weeks. Makes about 50 pita chips.

1 pita chip: 16 Calories; 0.7 g Total Fat (0.4 g Mono, 0.1 g Poly, 0.1 g Sat); 0 mg Cholesterol; 2 g Carbohydrate; 0 g Fibre; 0 g Protein; 26 mg Sodium

Pictured below.

Enliven your salads with fresh minty flavour and a poppy seed crunch. A tasty alternative to croutons.

tip

To toast sesame seeds, spread them in a single layer in an ungreased shallow pan. Bake in a 350°F (175°C) oven for 5 to 10 minutes, stirring or shaking often, until desired doneness. Don't be afraid to toast more than you need. Just freeze the extra in an airtight container for the next time.

Left: Minted Pita Chips, above
Right: Little Dilled Snacks, page 120

Great in your favourite salad or grilled cheese sandwich. Jean serves this as a salad on its own.

Marinated Onion Rings

Large red or white onion, sliced paper-thin (see Note) and separated into rings	1	1
Cold water		
Water	3/4 cup	175 mL
Granulated sugar	3/4 cup	175 mL
White vinegar	3/4 cup	175 mL
Cooking oil	1 tbsp.	15 mL
Salt	1/2 tsp.	2 mL
Pepper	1/8 tsp.	0.5 mL

Put onion rings into large heatproof bowl. Cover with cold water. Let stand for 1 hour. Drain.

Combine remaining 6 ingredients in small saucepan. Heat and stir on medium until boiling. Add to onion. Press onion with spoon into vinegar mixture. Cover. Chill for 24 hours to blend flavours. Store in refrigerator for up to 2 weeks. Serves 10.

1 serving: 82 Calories; 1.4 g Total Fat (0.8 g Mono, 0.4 g Poly, 0.1 g Sat); 0 mg Cholesterol; 18 g Carbohydrate; trace Fibre; 0 g Protein; 119 mg Sodium

Pictured on page 123.

Note: If you have one, an electric food slicer works best to achieve the thinnest possible onion slices.

Feta with red pepper, infused with savoury herbs and spices, makes a great salad topper.

Marinated Feta

Sprigs of fresh rosemary	3	3
Dried oregano	1 tbsp.	15 mL
Cumin seed	1 tbsp.	15 mL
Pepper	2 tsp.	10 mL
Red medium peppers, quartered	2	2
Cubed feta cheese	2 1/3 cups	575 mL
Olive (or cooking) oil	1/2 cup	125 mL

(continued on next page)

Combine first 4 ingredients in large bowl.

Arrange red pepper pieces, skin-side up, on ungreased baking sheet. Broil on top rack in oven for 10 to 15 minutes until skins are blistered and blackened. Transfer to small bowl. Cover with plastic wrap. Let sweat for about 15 minutes until cool enough to handle. Peel and discard skins (see Note). Cut into 1/3 inch (1 cm) slices. Add to rosemary mixture.

Add cheese and olive oil. Stir gently until coated. Transfer to airtight container. Marinate in refrigerator for at least 3 days to blend flavours, but no longer than 7 days. Drain and discard marinade. Makes about 2 cups (500 mL). Serves 12.

1 serving: 127 Calories; 11.1 g Total Fat (4.9 g Mono, 0.6 g Poly, 5 g Sat); 26 mg Cholesterol; 3 g Carbohydrate; trace Fibre; 4 g Protein; 327 mg Sodium

Pictured below.

Note: Prepared roasted red peppers are available in jars in most grocery stores. Drain well. Use in place of fresh, roasted red peppers.

Top: Marinated Feta, page 122
Bottom: Marinated Onion Rings, page 122

Throughout this book measurements are given in Conventional and Metric measure. To compensate for differences between the two measurements due to rounding, a full metric measure is not always used. The cup used is the standard 8 fluid ounce. Temperature is given in degrees Fahrenheit and Celsius. Baking pan measurements are in inches and centimetres as well as quarts and litres. An exact metric conversion is given on this page as well as the working equivalent (Metric Standard Measure).

Pans

Conventional – Inches	Metric – Centimetres
8 × 8 inch	20 × 20 cm
9 × 9 inch	22 × 22 cm
9 × 13 inch	22 × 33 cm
10 × 15 inch	25 × 38 cm
11 × 17 inch	28 × 43 cm
8 × 2 inch round	20 × 5 cm
9 × 2 inch round	22 × 5 cm
10 × 4 1/2 inch tube	25 × 11 cm
8 × 4 × 3 inch loaf	20 × 10 × 7.5 cm
9 × 5 × 3 inch loaf	22 × 12.5 × 7.5 cm

Oven Temperatures

Fahrenheit (°F)	Celsius (°C)	Fahrenheit (°F)	Celsius (°C)
175°	80°	350°	175°
200°	95°	375°	190°
225°	110°	400°	205°
250°	120°	425°	220°
275°	140°	450°	230°
300°	150°	475°	240°
325°	160°	500°	260°

Spoons

Conventional Measure	Metric Exact Conversion Millilitre (mL)	Metric Standard Measure Millilitre (mL)
1/8 teaspoon (tsp.)	0.6 mL	0.5 mL
1/4 teaspoon (tsp.)	1.2 mL	1 mL
1/2 teaspoon (tsp.)	2.4 mL	2 mL
1 teaspoon (tsp.)	4.7 mL	5 mL
2 teaspoons (tsp.)	9.4 mL	10 mL
1 tablespoon (tbsp.)	14.2 mL	15 mL

Cups

1/4 cup (4 tbsp.)	56.8 mL	60 mL
1/3 cup (5 1/3 tbsp.)	75.6 mL	75 mL
1/2 cup (8 tbsp.)	113.7 mL	125 mL
2/3 cup (10 2/3 tbsp.)	151.2 mL	150 mL
3/4 cup (12 tbsp.)	170.5 mL	175 mL
1 cup (16 tbsp.)	227.3 mL	250 mL
4 1/2 cups	1022.9 mL	1000 mL(1 L)

Dry Measurements

Conventional Measure Ounces (oz.)	Metric Exact Conversion Grams (g)	Metric Standard Measure Grams (g)
1 oz.	28.3 g	28 g
2 oz.	56.7 g	57 g
3 oz.	85.0 g	85 g
4 oz.	113.4 g	125 g
5 oz.	141.7 g	140 g
6 oz.	170.1 g	170 g
7 oz.	198.4 g	200 g
8 oz.	226.8 g	250 g
16 oz.	453.6 g	500 g
32 oz.	907.2 g	1000 g (1 kg)

Casseroles

Canada & Britain		United States	
Standard Size Casserole	Exact Metric Measure	Standard Size Casserole	Exact Metric Measure
1 qt. (5 cups)	1.13 L	1 qt. (4 cups)	900 mL
1 1/2 qts. (7 1/2 cups)	1.69 L	1 1/2 qts. (6 cups)	1.35 L
2 qts. (10 cups)	2.25 L	2 qts. (8 cups)	1.8 L
2 1/2 qts. (12 1/2 cups)	2.81 L	2 1/2 qts. (10 cups)	2.25 L
3 qts. (15 cups)	3.38 L	3 qts. (12 cups)	2.7 L
4 qts. (20 cups)	4.5 L	4 qts. (16 cups)	3.6 L
5 qts. (25 cups)	5.63 L	5 qts. (20 cups)	4.5 L

Tip Index

Recipe Index

most loved recipe collection most loved recipe collection